BURNING DESIRES

BURNING DESIRES

Jo Bannister

a&b

First published in paperback in Great Britain in 1996 by
Allison & Busby Ltd
179 King's Cross Road
London WC1X 9BZ

First published in hardcover by Macmillan London 1995

A catalogue record for this book is available from the
British Library

ISBN 0 74900 282 4

Printed and bound in Great Britain by
WBC Book Manufacturers, Bridgend, Mid Glamorgan

I

1

A rose bloomed in the darkness, tender orange and salmon-pink petals unfolding from its tight heart. It was only a tiny thing at first, a flower made of light blossoming in the black belly of a rotten building. But then with a soft explosion like an avid pant the bud of flame spread, and all at once there was a field of flowers – yellow and red and white – growing in the dark.

For a long moment the new-born fire was reflected in a pair of eyes, gleamed off teeth bared in a smile. Then the figure turned away, soft footsteps padded across the broken floor and a door opened and closed. After that there was just the fire, blooming and growing, and the urgent congress of little snaps and crackles as it debated its strategy.

No one called Detective Chief Inspector Frank Shapiro. No one was ready yet to say it was arson. There was no stench of petrol in the charred wreckage, no blackened fragments that could have been a timer, no reports of an intruder in the derelict warehouse. But Castlemere Fire Brigade could normally expect a major incident like this once a year and this was the second in four days. So while nobody was yet saying arson, everyone was thinking it. And while no one had called the head of Castlemere CID, Shapiro was nevertheless there.

It was Tuesday morning now, a pale October sunrise fighting its way through the sooty air. But when Shapiro was roused from his bed by siren after siren as every appliance Castlemere could muster raced across town to the warehouse in Viaduct Lane it was still Monday night, and he'd pulled on his warmest cardigan, a heavy tweed jacket he kept for the country walks he rarely took and his wellies. Also he needed a shave. With gloveless hands shoved in his pockets accentuating his naturally broad round-shouldered outline, in his comfortable old clothes and with a day's worth of greying stubble on his weary pensive face he looked like a tramp. A probationary fireman not long in Castlemere asked him if he'd been in the warehouse when it caught fire and if anyone else had been dossing there.

Leading Fireman Daniels interceded with a Cheshire cat grin, advised the embarrassed youth of his mistake and sent him off to rewind hoses. 'Sorry about that, Chief.'

Shapiro waved a tolerant hand. 'The last time my wife saw this jacket she said I'd be irresistible to a Salvation Army snatch squad. That was three years ago. I don't expect it's improved much since.'

The fire was out. It had taken four tenders and nearly four hours, and in the end it had died mostly of old age. Once the wooden floors had gone, the wooden rafters had charred to mere blackened ribs framing the sky and ten years of rubbish had blown away as ash on the smoky wind, there was nothing more for it to feed on and so it died.

Stone walls still reached up through three storeys: it would take a demolition crew to bring them down. But with no floors and no roof the building was finished. It dated back to the heyday of Victorian mercantile expansion, it had worked hard for a hundred years and stood idle for another ten, but four hours of fire and water had damaged it past repair. In another week there would be nothing here but a pile of smoke-blackened rubble. The demolition experts would move in as soon as it was safe to do so. After another team of experts had learned all they could from what remained.

'What do you think, Taff?' said Shapiro. 'A torch?'

Daniels squirmed inside his oilskin jacket. 'You'd need to ask the Governor that, Chief.'

'Of course,' agreed Shapiro. 'When he's not so busy. But what's your best guess?'

Daniels shrugged. 'Off the record? All the time we were in there we were looking out for late-firing incendiaries.'

Water was still coursing down the walls, dripping from the charred beams. It was too soon to begin a serious search for evidence, which would anyway be carried out by people with a more specific expertise than either DCI Shapiro or Leading Fireman Daniels. So they were talking gut feeling, no more. But Taff Daniels had seen a lot of fires and Frank Shapiro had seen a lot of crime, and the gut feeling of both was that either the fire at Rachid's Eight-Till-Late in Milne Road or this one could have been accidental but together they amounted to arson.

'Yes,' Shapiro agreed. 'Thanks, Taff. Tell your governor I'll call him later. There's nothing more I can do here.' He was standing in a morass of fine ash and water: when he moved his boots gave a mournful gurgle, echoing his feelings exactly.

It was almost half-past seven and Castlemere was beginning its working day. People who clocked on at eight had heard about the drama on the breakfast news and come out early to see for themselves. Behind the fire engines was a thick wall of sightseers. Not that there was much to see now. Those who rose early and were here before six were rewarded with great fountains of fire breaching the roof and the satisfying crash of masonry. Now the best on view was the devastation of fourteen thousand square metres of warehousing, which was impressive but not as thrilling as flames leaping into the night sky.

The firemen and Shapiro were not the only ones with more to do there than gawp. A reporter from the *Castlemere Courier* recognized him in spite of – or, disturbingly, because of – his informal attire and asked what she was to make of the presence of a detective chief inspector.

'Search me,' said Shapiro, 'I haven't had a report on this myself yet. Can I talk to you later, when I have?'

'If I call you about ten?'

'I might have something by then. At least whether we're looking for a careless smoker or a pyromaniac.'

She nodded. Her name was Gail Fisher, and she'd worked on other papers in other towns and knew that the price of a helpful DCI was above rubies. 'What about Rachid's shop? Is there a connection?'

Shapiro, who didn't wear glasses, looked at her as over the top of some. 'Ten o'clock did you say, Miss Fisher?'

She smiled, accepting her dismissal with a good grace. 'Ten o'clock, Chief.' She couldn't resist adding, 'But don't tell me you haven't wondered if you were too quick to write off Rachid's fire as an accident.'

Shapiro's expression was pained. 'We don't write off anything as anything, Miss Fisher. We try to find out what's happened. Rachid's was an empty shop with a rickety back entrance in an alley frequented by drunks: it seemed likely that the fire there wasn't deliberate. In the light of this' – he winced – 'of course we'll look again to see if we can learn anything more from Rachid's. But until the fire investigators tell me what happened here I can't say whether there's a connection or not. If you need a more positive quote than that you'd better make one up.'

'The same as usual, you mean?' They exchanged an amiable grin. 'I'll call you.' She went looking for firemen to interview.

Shapiro headed for his car. He wanted to go home and clean up before going to the office. But as he turned he saw something from the corner of his eye that was both familiar and out of place, though when he turned back to see what he couldn't immediately place it. The firemen tidying away their equipment, Gail Fisher talking to

Station Officer Silcott, a couple of photographers prowling the edges of the devastation exploding intermittent flashes, the wall of watching faces beginning to break up now the fun was over. Nothing remarkable.

Recognition hit him like a boot in the ribs and he sucked in a sharp breath. 'David?' He wasn't sure if he'd spoken aloud; certainly no one answered. Caught off guard, for some seconds he couldn't think what to do. His thick body swayed as if it wanted to continue with the day as planned, go home and then go to the office. He took a step towards the car. Then, ashamed of himself, he swung round and squelched after the slight figure weaving between the fire engines, light footed in filthy trainers.

The young man with the camera was seeking a way into the warehouse that wasn't guarded by firemen. A fire at its height is an awesome sight but a burnt-out building is just another kind of derelict until you go inside. He'd been here early enough to get the powerful shots of men on gossamer ladders silhouetted against the arching flames; now he wanted the companion piece of blackened rafters framing the morning. That meant getting inside, and that meant not being seen.

But when he passed behind the fire engines there wasn't a side door as he'd hoped; or rather, there had been until it was bricked up. With a muttered curse he turned on his heel, and almost walked into the man following him.

'David. What are you doing here?'

He was surprised but not that surprised. His face closed quickly, became wary and noncommittal. 'Working. Do I need CID's permission?'

Shapiro shook his head. 'No. But you do need to be careful. There's a lot of stuff in there could still come down.'

'I'll remember that.'

Shapiro sighed. Conversations with his son had been like this for as long as he could recall. There hadn't been many of them recently, but they were still all like this: verbal fencing between people too mistrustful to be rude. 'You're wet through. Have you been here all night?'

'Most of it.'

Shapiro despaired of getting any information from the young man. 'I'm going home – clean up, get some breakfast. Why don't you come? At least you could get dried out.'

David shook his head, just once, without taking his eyes off Shapiro. He hefted the camera. 'I have to develop these.'

'Later, then, if you have time. You know where I am.' Shapiro didn't wait for his son to make more excuses but turned and walked to his car; and the last thing he was thinking about was whether the warehouse in Viaduct Lane had been torched and, if so, by whom.

2

He spun out breakfast as long as he could but no one came so at nine fifteen he left for the office.

There was a message from Superintendent Taylor on his desk: when he had a moment would he pop downstairs? Shapiro straightened his tie in the mirror. He'd only had it on ten minutes but already the knot was under his ear. Superintendent Taylor's ties stayed put all day long. Shapiro didn't think his beard grew during office hours either.

Liz Graham was coming up the stairs as Shapiro descended. 'Good afternoon, Inspector,' he said pointedly.

She was inured to his gentle sarcasm. 'I just heard about Viaduct Lane. Anything I can do?'

'I'm not sure there's anything for any of us to do.'

'But with Rachid's—'

'I know, it makes you wonder. Silcott's got his people going over it: if they decide it's arson we'll need to take another look at Rachid's as well. In the mean time,' he added significantly, 'I have an interview with Sir.'

Liz was surprised. Superintendent Taylor didn't interfere much with CID. 'What does he want?'

'I don't know, but I could make an educated guess. He wants to know if it's occurred to me that the fire at Rachid's may not have been an accident after all.'

'I don't want to interfere,' said Superintendent Taylor. After thirty years of living and working in England he still strangled his vowels in a tortuously refined Edinburgh

9

accent. 'You know I don't like to interfere with your side of the business, Frank. There's no point having experts if you're going to tell them how to do their job.' He paused, his eyes keen, his head on one side, apparently waiting for some expression of gratitude.

Shapiro just said, 'No.' He had nothing against Taylor, except his ability to look smart at the end of a long day, but when they talked he never felt to be in the company of greatness. He had no worries about Taylor outsmarting him.

'I just wondered if you'd formed any opinion about last night's fire yet.'

'It's not a question of my opinion, sir. The Fire Brigade will tell me if there's likely to have been a crime.'

'Yes, of course. You haven't heard from them?'

Shapiro let Taylor see him looking at the clock over the mantelpiece. 'Hardly been time yet, sir. They only put the thing out a couple of hours ago. They'll want a good prowl round in daylight before they commit themselves.'

'Quite,' said Taylor. 'At least no one was hurt. There wasn't, was there – anyone hurt?'

'Not as far as I know. Unless they find bones when they start poking through the ashes.'

Along with his strangled vowels the Superintendent had rather refined sensibilities. He considered that in bad taste. 'No question of that, is there, Frank?' His manner was cool.

'There's always the possibility,' Shapiro said apologetically. 'We're not aware there's anyone missing, but Castlemere has as many tramps as any other middle-sized town and they all sleep somewhere. What we think is an empty building may be somebody's home. But they're not the sort of somebodies who'll be looked for when they don't turn up for work this morning.'

Aware that raising the issue had cost him Brownie points he decided to pre-empt the suggestion he felt sure

10

was coming. 'I thought I'd have another look at the shop fire in Milne Road on Friday night, see if there's any connection.'

'Rachid's?' Taylor's voice climbed. He seemed genuinely taken aback. 'Wasn't that an accident?'

Shapiro kept a straight face. 'Yes, probably.' He thought: Perhaps he's very good at making reports on time and keeping the expenses within budget. 'How are the wedding arrangements coming?'

Taylor darted him a hunted look. 'You've done this, haven't you? Your Rachael.' Shapiro nodded happily. 'Hell, isn't it?'

'Sheer hell. Still, only another week to go.'

'Another week of this and I'll be a nervous wreck,' said the father of the bride. 'And her mother'll go into withdrawal when she's finished shopping. You'll keep next Tuesday free?'

'Wouldn't miss it for the world,' Shapiro said truthfully. He hardly knew Taylor's children, wasn't sure he'd recognize them in the street. But he wanted to see if the man could get through his only daughter's wedding with his tie still in place.

When he got back to his office Liz was waiting. 'Silcott phoned.'

'And?'

'It probably was malicious. Nothing too sophisticated – no signs of a timer, anything like that. But the fire seems to have started simultaneously in three different places. There was no electricity in the warehouse, and it's hard to imagine three different dossers dropping three different cigarettes at the same time. So it looks like it was deliberate. And he said—'

'I know,' interrupted Shapiro wearily, 'I know. We should take another look at Rachid's.'

Before he left Queen's Street he spoke to Superintendent Taylor again and took Gail Fisher's call. 'We're treating the warehouse fire as malicious, and we're looking again at the fire in Milne Road on Friday night but it's too soon to say if there's a connection. As you know, we had no reason to believe there was anything suspicious about the first incident.'

'Do you know who owns the warehouse?'

Shapiro hadn't asked himself that. 'It's been derelict ten years: I suppose it belongs to someone but I don't know who.'

'I'm told it's owned by Hereward Holdings, which is in turn owned by Asil Younis through the Cornmarket Trading Company.'

From the way she said it, it was meant to convey more than it did. 'Yes. So?'

'Could that be the connection? That both properties were owned by immigrants?'

Then he realized what she was saying. 'You mean, some flower of Anglo-Saxon manhood who failed his GCSE in graffiti because he couldn't spell wog thinks a couple of Asian businessmen are lowering the tone of the neighbourhood?' Silence was her answer.

Shapiro wanted to say it was nonsense, she was looking for headlines where none existed. People in Castlemere were neither better nor worse than elsewhere, they had their virtues and their vices, but they'd never gone in for racism. They didn't take their children out of school when the number of permanent as against seasonal suntans reached some arbitrary threshhold, they didn't put pigs' trotters through the letterbox of the little mosque on Rosedale Road, and they'd never shown the sort of resentment that led to petrol-bombing small businesses. But the fact that it hadn't happened before didn't mean it couldn't happen now.

'In that case,' Shapiro said grimly, 'he'll be really cheesed off at being arrested by a Jew, won't he?'

The more he looked at the remains of Rachid's Eight-Till-Late, the more sure he was that Gail Fisher was mistaken. Not because there couldn't be a rabid racist with a box of firelighters in Castlemere, but because if there was he wouldn't have chosen Rachid's as a target. He could have done so much better.

For one thing the shop had been closed for six months, victim of a recession that had shut businesses up and down the country. The stock had been removed and the premises boarded up; all that remained to show it had been run by an Asian was a faded name over the shuttered window.

Also, it wasn't where it would attract attention. Though the address was Milne Road, in fact it was in a little alley off the thoroughfare: you had to know it was there to find it. Only a customer, of the shop or the cobbler's which shared the same alley, would be aware it was there. That meant if it was a racist it was a local racist, and most of the people in Milne Road had used the Eight-Till-Late and missed it when it closed.

The winos were another possibility. As a rule winos are too concerned with where the next bottle is coming from to worry about the colour of the man selling it. But the autumn frosts meant that people who had been happy pursuing their hobbies out of doors all summer were now seeking indoor venues: the back door of the shop would have been easy to force, and once inside the combination of drunks, spirits and roll-your-own fags was a recipe for disaster. The winos denied being inside Rachid's at all, but – as someone once observed in slightly different circumstances – they would, wouldn't they?

'No,' said Shapiro slowly, concluding several thoughtful minutes with a shake of his head. 'I don't believe it. I don't believe anyone burned either this shop or the Viaduct Lane warehouse because they used to be run by Asians. It makes no sense. A racist would burn thriving Asian businesses, not ones that were washed up and, in the case of the warehouse, where you'd have to search the Register of Companies to discover who the owner was

13

anyway. There's no name over the door there. To find Asil Younis you'd have to go through Hereward Holdings and Cornmarket Trading. Does that sound like a skinhead between soccer matches to you?'

Donovan said, 'Did they know each other?'

He had a reputation – among his other reputations – for being obscure but it wasn't often he left Shapiro floundering. 'Did who know who, Sergeant?'

'Rachid and Asil Thing. They're both – what, Pakistanis?'

Shapiro bristled just perceptibly. 'So?'

Donovan flashed his sudden alarming grin. 'Hey, Chief, we're all minorities here, OK? I know pretty well every Irishman in town, I guess you know every Jew, so maybe they knew each other too. If they did that's three things they had in common. No, four.'

'Four?'

'They come from the same community. They were both in business. They both had buildings that were excess to requirements, and now they're both expecting big cheques from the insurance.'

'Good God,' said Shapiro, genuinely surprised. 'You think they hired someone?'

'Could be. The first thing any minority learns is, you stick together. You want a teacher, a doctor, a lawyer or a son-in-law, you look to your own people. You need to talk about something as delicate as burning your premises for the insurance you do the same thing. If so, the guy they hired should be a Pakistani too.'

Shapiro was thinking. Mainly to fill the time while he was doing it he murmured, 'Isn't that contrary to the Fair Employment legislation?'

'Only if he put an advert in the paper,' said Donovan, deadpan.

People who'd known them for years still didn't understand the relationship between Detective Chief Inspector Shapiro and Detective Sergeant Donovan. Half of them

14

thought Shapiro could have found a better leg-man than a string-thin Irishman with an attitude problem, and the other half wondered how a restless spirit like Donovan could harness himself to a thirty-year man who'd already gone as far as he was going and whose primary interest these days must be his pension.

Both missed vital points. The problem with Cal Donovan's attitude was that he cared more about his work than most of the people he worked with so that frustration made him intolerant; while Shapiro had spent those thirty years honing his skills so that he could now think more quickly, deeply and intelligently than any detective on the division without breaking sweat.

The relationship worked because both men wanted it to and invested effort in it, and they drew dividends that were not always apparent to other people. Shapiro got his leg-work done by someone who cared about the results, and Donovan got to work with one of the unacknowledged masters of his profession.

Walking back to the car Shapiro changed the subject. 'How old are you, Sergeant?'

Donovan tried not to react every time his Chief Inspector surprised him. It would have left him time to do little else. 'Twenty-eight.'

'Ah. So you remember being twenty-three.'

'I started in CID when I was twenty-three.'

'That was around the time you came here, then.' Shapiro nodded pensively. 'Yes, you were a sullen little git as well.'

Donovan considered. 'This game we're playing, sir. Do I get to insult you in the second half?'

Shapiro chuckled apologetically. 'Sorry, Sergeant. It's my son. I'm trying to work out if he's just your average shiftless twenty-three-year-old or if he tries extra hard to annoy me. How did you get on with your family then?'

That got a reaction, if it was only shutters falling behind Donovan's dark, deep-set eyes. Everything about him was dark: the cast of his skin, his sense of humour, the clothes he wore, his habit of nursing a grievance. 'By the time I was twenty-three my family were dead.'

Shapiro winced. He'd have known that if he'd been thinking of anything beyond his own concerns. 'Sorry, lad. That was – clumsy.'

'It's all right.' The edge of bitterness glinted and was gone from Donovan's tone. 'It's history. But it means I can't help you. Try Inspector Graham, she still sees her father.'

'Girls are different,' Shapiro said lugubriously. 'I have no trouble with my girls. But David's always been a puzzle to me. He lives in London now, takes photographs for magazines or something. He was at this morning's fire. I didn't even know he was in town.'

'Where's he staying?'

'I don't know.' A man accustomed to controlling the activities of others, he seemed disturbed because he couldn't control those of his son.

'Are you worried about him?'

'I don't know,' said Shapiro again, impatiently. 'I haven't seen him for eighteen months; I haven't heard from him since Chanukkah. Now he's here and it's only by accident that I find out. I don't know why he behaves like that.'

'You said the reason. He's twenty-three.'

They'd reached the car. Shapiro sighed. 'What the hell, I have other children who appreciate me even if he doesn't.'

Donovan grinned.

'Right,' said Shapiro briskly. 'The fires. Rachid: find out who he is, and if he's still in the area go talk to him. I'll see Mr Younis, find out if he needed the money tied up in the warehouse. But a Pakistani torch? I still can't see it.'

Donovan shrugged like a black heron rattling its feathers. 'I don't see why not. Crime is colour-blind.'

'Oh, I like that,' snorted Shapiro. 'You should get that framed. Look lovely on your desk, that would.' Shapiro had a photograph of his ex-wife and his daughters on his. Liz Graham had a small one of her husband and a large one of her horse. Donovan often had a part stripped from his motorbike, but problems had yet to arise with his new machine so for now the only thing pinning down his paperwork was more paperwork.

'What about the winos from Rachid's? I could talk to them again.'

'Would you know where to find them?'

'They're my new neighbours.' Donovan didn't sound as appalled as most householders would but then he didn't live on a narrow boat for the gentility of the area. 'Saturday morning they moved into the alley beside the timberyard.'

'Yes, all right. See if they remember seeing any strangers hanging round the shop before the fire.'

'It'll be something if they remember the fire,' said Donovan with a quirk of grim humour.

3

The winos began to appear after the timberyard shut at six, though the gathering wouldn't be complete and the serious business of the evening under way until the sun set half an hour later. Dusk came quickly in these urban canyons; only on the canal did the day linger another quarter of an hour, its last pink rays picking out the primary colours on the houseboats moored along the bank.

Some of them, like Donovan's, were proper narrow boats built to carry cargo on the inland waterways. Others were essentially floating caravans. Together they formed an oddly cohesive little community in one of the more depressed parts of Castlemere; never more so than after the sun went down, when the brightness of their paint and the glow of their curtained windows made an island of suburbia in the black heart of an industrial area that was only a step from dereliction.

Once the timberyard and the adjacent garden centre closed the only activity on the wharf was the boat dwellers coming home, and they knew better than to poke around in the alleys. So the winos were safe from interference; except from people like Donovan.

He waited until the light was fading, judging that they would open up after sunset, then padded the short distance up the wharf to the alley. The last of the day went as he stepped over the threshold from dusk into darkness.

His eyes adjusting, he picked out the shapes of five

18

men among the piles of waste lumber. He approached soft footed and heard the drone of voices before they realized he was there and fell abruptly silent.

Among the five were two he recognized, from the general outline and the sound of their voices, as having come from Rachid's. He spoke to them after the shop fire when they were still worried about where they would go. Now they gazed up at him with the same mixture of anxiety and fatalism spiced by a dash of hostility, sure he was bad news but still confident he wouldn't be worse news than they'd heard before.

Rather than loom over them he leaned back against a stack of pallets, his hands in his pockets and his ankles crossed. 'Remember me?'

Someone grunted, 'Oh yeah,' as if it were not a compliment.

Donovan nodded at the timber. 'Your last place burned down. I hope you'll be more careful here.'

The man who'd grunted said, 'Nothing to do with us, that.'

'Coincidence, then,' said Donovan sardonically. 'The nights are getting colder, you need somewhere to warm up, the place you've been boozing all summer burns down, but it's all a coincidence.' He sniffed. 'Maybe someone burned it for the insurance.'

They resented his attitude but didn't know what to do about it. 'Could be,' said the spokesman. 'There's people about, even after dark. You don't have to blame us for everything that happens.'

'What people?'

'Nobody in particular,' said the man defensively. 'But the way you tell it, nobody was ever up that alley but us, and that's not true. Anybody could have dropped a match.'

'You saw someone?'

'Don't remember.'

Donovan breathed heavily. 'If it wasn't you there must

19

have been someone else there, and if there was you'd have seen him. Did you?'

'Hard to say. Had a bottle, didn't we?'

'So maybe there was no one there but you. In which case—'

'Sergeant,' another of the men interrupted in a clear, faintly exasperated voice that took Donovan by surprise, 'you've asked him that four times now, and four times he's answered you. Are you going to keep asking until he makes something up to get rid of you?'

There wasn't enough light to see faces: if they meant to make a fire for the warmth they hadn't got round to it yet. But it was a young man's voice; and not a dosser's voice, it wasn't rusty enough and there was no burr of alcohol on it. He wasn't one of the group, even though he was sitting cross-legged among them with his hair hanging in his face and one knee coming out of his jeans. Looking more closely Donovan saw that what the man was cradling in his lap, that he'd taken for a bottle, was something quite different.

'Let me guess. David Shapiro.'

The young man uncurled, rising fluidly to his feet. He sounded surprised and slightly aggrieved. 'How do you know?'

'I'm a detective.'

The young man laughed at that, a laugh as clear as a bell. 'And?'

'And your da mentioned seeing you,' admitted Donovan.

'You work for him?'

Donovan nodded, introduced himself.

The winos were getting restless. They'd come here for a bit of privacy, not to be bombarded with questions and threatened with photography. Somebody said, 'You never said you had a camera.' Somebody else said, 'I'm off.' There was an undignified scramble and thirty seconds later Donovan and David Shapiro had the alley to themselves.

'Now look what you've done,' Donovan said philosophically. 'Want some coffee?'

David looked round the shut buildings and the rotting ones. 'Where?'

'My place.' He led the way.

David was enchanted by the narrow boat. He prowled round opening cupboards. 'How long have you had her?'

'A few years. I inherited the family farm. Well, I'd no use for twenty acres of dirt in Ireland so I sold it and bought *Tara*.'

'No regrets? No yearning for the ancestral soil?'

'No.'

'Then why'd you call her *Tara*?'

Donovan gave a saturnine smile. 'Coffee's ready.'

When David stopped prowling and sat under the light in the saloon, Donovan wasn't surprised he'd been able to pass as a wino. He was unshaven, his hair was tangled, his clothes were tattered and dirty and he looked cold. If Donovan hadn't guessed who he was he'd probably have arrested him on suspicion of stealing the camera. 'What are you doing here?'

David shrugged. He had the height and build of a teenage boy rather than a grown man and a quick, tense way of moving. 'Working. Or trying to. The job I came here to do has taken himself off for a week's badger watching in Cumbria and I'm supposed to cool my heels till he gets back.'

'Badgers?' Donovan made it sound like an expletive.

David grinned, a pinched edgy grin without much humour. 'Keaton Payne, the naturalist. I'm taking photographs for a magazine that's serializing his new book. Only when I turn up on his doorstep, all at once there's been a misunderstanding and he's on his way to Cumbria.'

'What did your magazine say to that?'

'That's the problem,' said David ruefully, 'it's not my magazine. I'm freelance – they hire me when they can use me, kiss me off when they can't. So what they said is,

21

if there's no subject there's no job. If I want to hang around till he gets back that's up to me.'

'Tough.'

'Tell me about it.' David finished his coffee as if it was the first hot drink he'd had all day. 'Payne was supposed to be putting me up. I can't afford a week in a hotel.'

'What about your da?'

The smile was barbed. 'I'm not prepared to pay what that'd cost me either.'

'Stay here then,' said Donovan off-handedly. 'There's a spare cabin. Or there will be if I put the engine back together.'

David's sharp face was hopeful. 'Do you mean that?'

'Sure. Why not?'

The boy was on his feet like a shot. 'I'll get my van. It's up on Brick Lane. I've been sleeping in it since Saturday. Tell you one thing: this town hasn't got any warmer in the last three years.'

Donovan watched him go with a fractional, barely conscious shake of the head. He knew Shapiro's house, knew there were empty rooms, wondered how things had got so strained between them that David would rather sleep in the back of a van than in his father's home.

When he'd reassembled the engine, watching David stow his gear – two padded cases for the cameras and lenses and a small grip for his clothes – he said, 'What were you doing with the winos?'

'Trying to get their confidence,' David said, his lips making an ironic curve. 'Till you came along.'

'Gee, sorry,' Donovan said insincerely. 'You want to photograph them? Why? I don't expect they started that fire, you know.'

'The first I knew of any fire was when you mentioned it. No, I'm trying to put together a portfolio. Anything interesting or dramatic, anything in the news.' His voice warmed. 'That's what I want to do: news photography. There aren't too many openings, you need to be able to show you're good. Well, I am, and when I've got the shots to prove it all the badger watchers in Britain won't be worth an hour of my time. Beirut, Jerusalem, Sarajevo, Mogadishu – that's where I'm going.' A ring of challenge crept into his tone. 'Don't you believe me?'

Donovan didn't understand the hostility that lurked just under the surface, waiting to be scratched. 'Sure I believe you. But I still don't see where the winos fit in.'

'Homelessness: one of the big issues of the Caring Nineties. Plus, they have the sort of faces that work in black and white.'

'What else have you got for this portfolio?'

'Do you want to see it?' Enthusiastic as a child he rooted through one of the cases. 'There's stuff in there as good as anything you'll see in the papers.'

Donovan was no expert but he thought the boy was probably right. It was powerful material, heavily chiaroscuro, dramatic in content and presentation. Lined faces hopeless with poverty, mean streets cut off by the tide of time: stark images that seemed the very antithesis of sentimentality yet tugged some internal thread of guilt. Of course Donovan, being Irish, was born sentimental. Only sheer hard work had earned him a reputation as a ruthless bastard.

'And our winos were going in here?'

'If they were good enough. It's hard to be sure always when you're taking them. But yes, that's what I had in mind.'

After the seamed faces and streets came an abrupt change of mood. One minute Donovan was voyeur at a depressed inner-city mission where the hymns were the price of the supper, the next he was plunged into the depths of a riot. Angry faces, screaming faces, thudding fists and feet were everywhere. Donovan, who'd seen riots at first hand, felt an unpleasant jolt in the pit of his stomach. 'How did you get that without getting flattened?'

'Telephoto lens,' said David. 'I'm keen, not suicidal.'

23

A catalogue of dramas followed the riot. A motorway pile-up: first the conventional overhead shot from a bridge showing the full scope of the incident but making it look as if someone had dropped a box of toy cars, then the same episode from hubcap level focused on the immediate human and mechanical carnage. A gas explosion that had made the street erupt like a volcano, a fractured water main fountaining through the crater. A coaster breaking her back on a sandbank, unheeded by children playing on the beach.

Donovan nodded slowly. 'They are good. Who've you showed them to?'

David gave an edgy chuckle. 'So far? You. A couple of friends. Nobody. It's not finished yet. When it's finished I'll show it to every picture editor from Fleet Street to Wapping.'

'What are you waiting for? It looks pretty comprehensive to me.'

'But you're not an editor, are you? I don't know, it needs – some sort of climax, something special. I'll know it when I see it, then Keaton Payne can go to hell.' He looked up then, a sheen in his eyes that was half anger, half humour. 'Want to hear something silly?'

'Go on.'

'The badgers were an excuse. He didn't want a Jew in his house.'

'How do you know?'

'He only remembered he had urgent business elsewhere after I told him my name.'

They eyed one another levelly, then Donovan began to chuckle. After a half-offended moment David joined in. 'What's so funny? I've spent four days living in a van because some WASP ferret fancier doesn't want me contaminating his home. What's so frigging funny about that?'

Still laughing, Donovan shook his head. 'When he gets back from Cumbria, try again. Clean up, put on a tie: he

24

won't recognize you. Tell him Mr Shapiro couldn't wait so the magazine sent you instead. Tell him your name's Seamus O'Flynn.'

'*Why?*'

'Then you'll see what a bum's rush is really like.'

In the middle of the night, sleeping as he often did, not in his bed but on it, a book propped against his knees, Donovan was jerked awake by sudden mayhem of shouts, running feet, clutching hands. For a crazy moment before he was alert enough to understand he was in the midst of that riot again, trampled under surges of hatred and panic.

Then his mind cleared enough for him to remember where he was and know that it was David Shapiro shaking his arm as if lives depended on it. 'Wha—?' he mumbled. 'What's the matter? What's that—?' His wits sharpened as he registered unexpected light and impossible colours flickering against the bedroom curtain.

'Fire!' yelled David. His sharp face was alight with excitement, his voice vibrant with it. 'The timberyard across the way. It's gone up like a Roman candle.'

4

Before he went topsides Donovan called the Fire Brigade and Queen's Street. Then he hurried on deck.

The sound and the smell reaching down the companionway prepared him for the sight of the fire. The roar of it was like an army on the march, feet and voices and the creak of equipment crammed together in an urgent shapeless chaos of sound. The smell was like walking into a wall, acrid and pungent and so thick there was no saying where the smell left off and the smoke began.

So he was ready for something spectacular; but he was still startled by just how spectacular, how comprehensive, a blaze it was. He froze half out of the hatch, and he knew his mouth was open because he could taste the smoke, but for long stunned seconds he seemed powerless to move.

Fire coated half the sky, leaping up the black sphere and pouring smoke the colour of gunmetal to blot out the few brave stars. There are many flammable substances in a sawmill: resin-rich timber, piles of shavings, drums of preservative. People who sell timber take precautions so there are fewer timberyard fires than there might be. But there are no small ones.

So far as Donovan could see the building was ablaze from end to end. Lumber piled in the alley was burning too, and as he watched the windows of the adjacent garden centre imploded with a sound like musical shellfire, victims of the blistering heat.

26

'David?'

He looked both ways along the wharf and there was all the light he needed to see there was no one on the tow-path. But there was movement on the other boats now as the noise brought sleepers from their beds. *Tara* and *James Brindley* were nearest to the fire, both too close for comfort.

Martin Cole's head appeared out of the *Brindley*'s doghouse and Donovan, vaulting on to the tow-path, shouted to him. 'Fire Brigade's on its way. But you'd better move: if that building comes down it'll throw bricks clean across the canal.'

Cole yelled back, 'What about *Tara*?'

Donovan didn't let himself wonder. 'She'll have to take her chances. Did you see someone – young feller with a camera?'

Cole was already bent over his bow warp, working it loose. 'Nobody came this way.'

'God-damn.' Two things Donovan was afraid of: facing that fire, edging up on it with the heat searing his eyes, looking into its furious dancing heart, knowing that at any moment it would boil up out of its brick cauldron and spew hot rubble like lava over all the surrounding wharf, in order to find a photographer who wanted a spectacular climax for his CV; and facing said photographer's father and admitting that he hadn't dared search for him.

That swung it. He owed Shapiro, hadn't time to work out how much.

He needed to get to Broad Wharf. David wasn't on the tow-path, and if he'd gone into the alley he was beyond help. The other places you could photograph the fire from were Broad Wharf, where the tow-path opened into an unloading dock on the far side of the timberyard, and Brick-Lane, which ran along the back and was reached by a walkway from the same place. To reach Broad Wharf he'd have to chance the narrow tow-path with the building blazing above him.

Donovan was afraid of fire. Not irrationally afraid: he knew exactly what it could do. It destroyed things and people, destroyed them as if they had never been. At the same time there was an unpredictability about it that was almost human. It was impossible to judge how many liberties you could take with it. Provided he was cool and agile enough, a man might dart in front of a runaway train and know that as long as he cleared the track one second before the engine reached him the worst he would suffer would be a buffeting from the slipstream. It wouldn't find an extra burst of speed from somewhere, it wouldn't reach out for him, if it missed him first time it wouldn't throw itself sideways in order to get him that way.

Fire could do all those things and more. It was more like a live enemy than a physical phenomenon. Indeed, any comprehensive definition of life would include fire, and to Donovan that seemed fair enough. That was how it felt to face a fire: like going into battle against a hostile power that had intelligence, strength and weapons of incalculable capacity at its disposal.

None of which altered the situation. To search for David Shapiro with some hope of finding him he had to reach Broad Wharf, and the only way of doing that without a lengthy detour was to pass behind the burning building and trust that even if the wall was going to come down it wouldn't do it in the ten seconds it would take him. He packed his lungs with smoky air, gritted his teeth and hurled himself into the heat and the danger like a sprinter coming off his blocks.

Halfway – too far from the end, too late to go back – he thought he'd guessed wrong and the wall could come down in less than ten seconds. A roar and a gout of flame above him broke his stride and made him duck, throwing his arm up in a fatuous gesture of self-defence. But it wasn't the wall, it was the roof that had gone, charred beams and superheated tin crashing into the furnace

28

below. Donovan ran on and reached the comparative safety of Broad Wharf, where the air was only as hot as a hair-dryer and only as thick as a puff on a Turkish cigar.

He didn't have to look for David. While he was still bent double fighting for breath David appeared at his side, flames dancing in his eyes like wine. He had his camera in one hand and waved it with scant respect for its delicate insides. 'Did you ever *see* anything like *this*?' he shouted over the roar.

Donovan didn't know whether to be glad he was safe or furious that he'd risked his neck to find out. He stayed where he was, bent double, breathing heavily.

Sirens in Brick Lane heralded the arrival of the fire engines. Under the cover of water jets, figures in black and yellow oilskins trotted through the walk-way bringing more hoses with them.

'Away out of there, lads,' one of them shouted, the accent instantly identifying Leading Fireman Daniels. Then he peered through the smoke. 'What – Donovan, is it? What you doing here?'

'Nothing,' said Donovan, straightening. 'We're just going.'

David was indignant. 'I'm not finished yet.'

'Oh yes you are,' Donovan said with conviction.

That was when the wall went. It may have been the pressure of the water pouring into the building, it may have been that with the roof gone there was nothing left to hold it together; it may have been that the fire took just that amount of time to do its work. But the wall backing on to the canal began to belly out, as if it were made of rubber, and then – almost in slow motion – it fell.

'Watch yourselves!' yelled Daniels.

But the wall wasn't heading for Broad Wharf, it was falling over the tow-path. Donovan watched stunned as the masonry broke up, filling the air with a lethal hail of sparks and hot brick.

He wasn't a man who put a lot of himself into possessions. Mostly he bought things when he needed them, kept them while they were useful and disposed of them when they were finished with. Apart from his one suit and not-quite-matching tie for formal occasions, he chose his clothes for warmth, comfort and proximity to the store entrance. His music system was so basic it came in one box marked Cassette Player, and the remote control for his television was a long stick.

There were really only two things he made any emotional investment in. As luck would have it his bike, because it was new and he was still protecting it from the harsh realities of life on the tow-path, was in the garage at Queen's Street with a *Fingerprints: Do Not Touch* sign on it. But his boat was moored within spitting distance of the building, and he didn't know what he'd see when the dust cleared.

He saw nothing. For a moment he thought there must still be too much rubbish in the air, that he wasn't seeing as far up the wharf as he thought. But the more the dust settled, the clearer the view of the rubble piled high on the tow-path and spilling into the canal, the surer he was that he could see everything there was to be seen. And there was no sign of *Tara*. No battered hulk strewn with bricks. No superstructure half-sunk in the murky water. Nothing he recognized floating on the boiling, scummy surface even. She was gone as if she had never existed.

'Oh, shit.'

David touched his arm. 'There.'

Beyond the rubble, beyond the arena lit by the manic glow of the fire, something was moving on the dark water. The throb of an engine reached them over the roar of flames.

'That's the *Brindley*, Martin Cole's boat. Oh—' He saw it too, the long dark shape skewing awkwardly behind the *James Brindley* because there was no one at the tiller.

The high pitch of a woman's voice carried to them where a man's wouldn't have. Even so they couldn't hear every word: 'warps' was one and 'sorry' another.

'What's she saying?'

Donovan knew because he knew what must have happened. 'She's apologizing for cutting my warps. They hadn't time to untie her: they cut her loose, got a rope on her and towed her clear.' She couldn't, he knew, have escaped scot-free. There'd be the warps to replace. He'd be lucky if at least some of the flying bricks hadn't found her windows. Her varnish would be scarred by cinders and he'd probably have to repaint to get rid of the soot. But he still had a home.

'You know,' David Shapiro said in all seriousness as they retreated from the danger zone, 'you should have moved her before you came to look at the fire.'

There was a council of war in the DCI's office at eight o'clock. Shapiro was grim. 'Well, we suspected before but after this there can't be any doubt. It's arson. I'm not even going to consider the possibility of three major fires in a week, all of them accidents.'

'I don't know how else to put this,' said Donovan, his face devoid of expression. 'But is there a coloured gentleman in the woodpile?'

Detective Inspector Graham didn't understand, looked at him blankly. 'What?'

With a faint smile Shapiro explained. 'The two previous fires were on premises owned by Pakistanis. Sergeant Donovan's wondering about the timberyard.' He pulled a printout across the desk towards him. 'But according to this the place is owned by assorted members of the Evans family. An Evans founded it and his grandsons are the current owners.' One eyebrow twitched sardonically. 'Not a lot of Pakistanis called Evans, are there, Sergeant?'

'Not a lot, sir, no,' said Donovan, deadpan.

'What were you thinking?' asked Liz. 'Attacks on immigrant businesses?'

'Could be. We also wondered, since both the previous

31

attacks were on defunct businesses, if it was for the insurance and the torch was someone known to both Asil Younis of Hereward Holdings and Rachid—'

'Rachid Aziz,' supplied Donovan, 'aged thirty-seven, of Flat 3, 102 Rosedale Road.'

'And Rachid Aziz of Rachid's Eight-Till-Late off Milne Road,' Shapiro finished seamlessly. 'But the Evans family rather upset that calculation, in more ways than one. Not only are the owners not Pakistanis, their business was thriving – it's hard to see why they'd prefer to have the insurance. There may be a connection that we haven't thought of yet. Or the only connection may be that these three places were handy when someone who gets a kick out of fires happened along.'

'So who do we talk to and what do we ask?'

'The owners,' decided Shapiro. 'It's the only line we can pursue till we turn something up. Donovan's going to see Rachid and I was going to talk to Mr Younis. Could you take that over, Liz? I've got to go and see Sir when he gets in.'

Liz chuckled. In the portly, sonorous, mid-fifties Detective Chief Inspector there remained traces of the schoolboy. She amused herself with the image of him waiting outside Superintendent Taylor's office twisting his cap in his hands. 'About this?'

'I expect so,' said Shapiro. 'What else?'

As they split up he signalled Donovan to wait. 'About last night. I don't know why David was staying with you when I've got a bed for him at home. But it looks to me – from what you've told me, and what I was told by the Fire Brigade who were rather more forthcoming, not to mention displeased – that my son's actions were the direct cause of the damage to your boat.'

'The fire,' Donovan said, 'was the direct cause of the damage to my boat. Such as it is. I'll fix it up come the weekend.'

Shapiro wasn't satisfied. 'It was David's fault you hadn't

32

time to move it before the building fell on it.'

'If I hadn't been looking for David I'd have been looking for whoever started the fire, or making sure there was no one else in danger. With or without David, the boat was always going to be a low priority.'

'All the same, I don't want you out of pocket.'

'I won't be. That's what insurance is for. That's why I pay the premium every year. Stop worrying, Chief, everything's fine.'

'What about tonight? I can put you both up if you can't stay there.'

Donovan rolled his eyes. 'Tell you what, Chief. If I need a piece of cardboard for the window I'll come straight to you. Otherwise, forget it.' With that he left, closing the door behind him.

Shapiro sighed, disappointed. He'd hoped for a windfall out of this, that he'd get his son under his own roof for a few days. But David wouldn't come unless Donovan did, and pride stopped him putting it to his sergeant like that.

The phone rang. Station Officer Silcott was tired after his night's exertions, but more than that he sounded grim. 'It's just got nasty, Frank.'

'It is arson, then.'

'Oh, it's arson all right, but that's not what I meant. We've found a body. Someone was sleeping under the pallets in the alley – dosser, probably, though there wasn't much left for an ID. Poor sod never had a chance. I guess that makes it a minimum of manslaughter.'

5

Rachid Aziz had a wife, two daughters, a flat rather too small for them, an elderly hatchback and a job stacking supermarket shelves that was whittling away, pound by pound, the debts incurred when his own shop failed.

'What was the problem?' asked Donovan. 'A corner shop like that: you might never get rich but I wouldn't have thought you'd have gone bust either.'

'I was unlucky,' said Mr Aziz, his eyes low as if confessing a sin. 'I borrowed money to buy the shop. Then the interest rates went up so all my profit went to cover the debt. Then the council demolished three streets of small houses on the far side of Milne Road and erected a bus station and a multi-storey car park. No doubt these are most useful facilities but they don't buy groceries the way three streets of small houses did.'

'When did you close?'

'I tried to sell the business first,' said Aziz. 'But it was obvious to all that if I couldn't make it pay neither could anyone else. Then I tried to sell the building. Only prices had dropped twenty per cent since I bought it so even if I found a buyer I would still be in debt. I played for time, hoping the recession would end. But it got worse, and then I couldn't sell the shop at all. Little businesses like mine were closing all over the country, who was going to put their money into one now? Finally I had no choice but to seek work elsewhere and let the shop lie empty.

This was in April.' He smiled sadly. 'At the end of the financial year.'

Donovan did the sum. 'And after six months you were still looking for a buyer and still paying the interest on your loan?'

'Oh, yes. It is not easy, but then neither was running the shop. At least with the supermarket I know how much money I will have at the end of each week.'

'It must have been a relief when the place burned down,' suggested Donovan.

Aziz met his eyes. 'Oh, yes. It was of course insured as a condition of the loan. Because the market value has fallen the insurance company will not pay out the full amount, but it will pay off most of my debt. By working hard I will pay the rest.'

Donovan pursed his lips and wondered how to phrase the next question. Rachid Aziz saved him the trouble. 'So now you are wondering if I went there on Friday night with a can of petrol and a box of matches, and solved my problems that way. Yes?'

'Yes,' admitted Donovan.

'The answer, Sergeant Donovan, is no. If you ask if I am pleased, then the answer to that is that I am very pleased. If you ask how long I could have managed had something like this not happened, the answer is not very long and I was most dreadfully worried. If you ask whether it had occurred to me to burn my shop, then I have to confess that it had, more than once.

'And still I tell you that I did not do it, that I do not know who did, that I never paid anyone to do it and never asked anyone to do it. And if you ask why you should believe me when there seems every reason not to, all I can say is that I did not do it and never would have done it because it would be wrong.'

Donovan's instinct was to believe him. He saw many people in the course of his work, many of them crooked, some of them dumb enough to be obvious crooks, some of them clever enough to make you wonder. But he thought Rachid Aziz wasn't even one of those so much as an honest man.

However, he'd been a policeman long enough to know that no amount of intuition was a substitute for evidence. 'Where were you on Friday night? Between finishing work and about midnight when the fire started.'

Aziz cast his mind back, gave an apologetic shrug. 'I was at home, with my family. They will confirm this. But you would not expect them to say I was out burning down my shop.'

So he had to settle for intuition after all. 'OK, Mr Aziz. I'll probably want to see you again at some point, but I don't expect you're planning on leaving the country, are you?'

Aziz risked a little smile. 'Not until the insurance on my shop comes through.'

As he was leaving another question occurred to Donovan. 'Do you know Mr Asil Younis at all?'

The open countenance of Mr Aziz shut like a box. Ice cracked in his voice. 'Indeed I do not.'

Donovan raised an eyebrow. 'And don't want to, by the sound of it. Why, what's wrong with him?'

Aziz's lips were tightly compressed and for a moment he resisted answering. Then he relented. 'Sergeant Donovan, Mr Younis is a very successful businessman. He came to this country with nothing, now he is a wealthy man with a big house in the best part of Cambridge Road. His sons are successful also, and he made for his daughter a good marriage. He is a most generous benefactor of our mosque. These things notwithstanding, Sergeant, Mr Younis is not a good man.'

This was all news to Donovan. 'You mean he's a crook?'

Aziz gave a little shake of the head. 'That I cannot say, not knowing the details of his business activity. All I can say is that Mr Younis is not a man whose company I would seek. Not a man whose family I would wish my family to associate with.'

Donovan scratched his head but couldn't get Aziz to say more. When asked how he'd formed this opinion of a man he didn't know, all he would say was that as members of the same small community they naturally heard things about one another that outsiders would not. Asked if he knew anything about Mr Younis that the police should know, Mr Aziz would go no further than repeating that Mr Younis was not a good man.

Donovan knew better than to beat his head against a stone wall. He left Aziz standing stiffly by the mantelpiece, unconsciously fiddling with the photographs.

The house on Cambridge Road was about as grand as a house can be before people start talking snidely of stately homes. It was between-the-wars Palladian, with a Portland stone colonnade forming the frontage. A blink of aquamarine through the windows on one side of the pedimented doorcase suggested a swimming-pool. In front of the house the gravel drive made a graceful sweep round a circle of manicured lawn featuring a bronze sundial on a marble plinth.

To go with all this Liz expected a butler. But when she said who she was and asked to see Mr Younis, the small man in the dark suit who answered the door held it wide and said, 'I am Asil Younis, Inspector Graham, how may I help you?'

He showed her to a sitting-room where they talked without interruption. Indeed, for all she could hear to the contrary they might have been alone in the house.

She came directly to the point. 'Monday night's fire at your warehouse. We're treating it as malicious.'

'Yes,' said Asil Younis.

'You're not surprised?'

He gave a delicate Asiatic shrug. 'The Fire Brigade said it probably was.'

She felt a momentary twinge of annoyance. 'Yes, of course. Now you've had the chance to think about it, have you any idea who might have been responsible?'

Younis looked surprised. He had very dark eyes set deep into a smooth dark skin. Liz found it impossible to judge his age: he could have been anywhere between about forty and fifty-five. He said, 'I supposed vagrants . . .' His voice too was ambivalent. There were enough shades of difference that you knew it wasn't an English voice, not enough remaining of his native accent to place it accurately.

'With three fires in five days,' said Liz, 'we think it's rather more deliberate than that. Is there anyone who might have a grudge against you, Mr Younis? Either you personally or one of your companies?'

'Undoubtedly,' said Asil Younis, smiling. 'That, Inspector, is the price of success. It's easy to have friends as long as you aren't too good at your job.'

'And who might have been sufficiently aggrieved by your success to put a match to your property?'

'No one at all,' said Younis firmly. 'Don't misunderstand me, Inspector. I have plenty of – enemies may be too strong a word, but people who have no fondness for me. It is possible that one among them might take direct action to embarrass me. But none of them would have chosen to burn that warehouse. For one thing, it would not be common knowledge that it belonged to me. Even in the business community, only someone with a long memory would know that when that building was in use it was run by Hereward Holdings which is a wholly owned subsidiary of my company Cornmarket Trading. None of this is secret, you understand, but it is of no interest who owns a derelict building.

'And the other reason none of my enemies would destroy it is that I would count it a favour. I haven't found a use or a buyer for that property in ten years. It is an embarrassment to me. I am most pleased that it is gone. I shall be even more pleased when the insurance pays out. Oh no, Inspector Graham, no one burned that building out of hatred for me.' He smiled again, a small feline

38

smile that Liz couldn't interpret. 'And I don't think I have any friends kind enough to burn it for love.'

She had long ago learned to give nothing away by her expression. She might be puzzled by this clever, articulate, wealthy man; she might be unsure how to judge nuances of tone and gesture that would mean one thing in a home-grown man of the same age and status and something quite different in one of another culture; she might wish there was someone whose opinion she respected she could compare notes with afterwards. But outwardly she remained composed and in control of the situation. She couldn't match Shapiro's wonderfully impervious Upholder-of-the-Queen's-Peace mien: she wasn't equip-ped, lacking the breadth of face to pin it on or the number of chins needed to support it. Nor could she yet match the gymnastic agility of the brain masked by that stolid expression. But she was a skilful detective who conducted a sound and comprehensive interview, and if she were unsure how to react to Asil Younis she could at least keep him from guessing that.

She said calmly, 'Which raises the other point we have to consider. Could it have been done by someone in your employ?'

Younis laughed out loud, amused by her directness. 'You're asking if I torched my own warehouse for the insurance?'

'It would be useful to have your response to that, sir, yes.'

'The answer, Inspector, is no.'

'I see,' said Liz. 'Could someone working for you have done it without your knowledge – thinking he was doing you a favour, perhaps?'

'No, Inspector. People who work for me don't do any-thing without my knowledge. I encourage obedience over initiative. I have enough initiative for us all.'

'I'd be safe assuming, then, that if the act was carried out by someone on your staff the order came from you.'

Younis's smile grew broad. 'Inspector, I believe you would. But you will waste altogether too much time looking for this imaginary employee. My advice is that you look for your arsonist elsewhere.'

Liz gave a friendly nod. 'Oh, we will, sir. We'll be looking for him in all sorts of places. We'll turn him up. Hopefully before he damages any more of your fellow-countrymen's property.'

For the first time Younis frowned. 'My—? Inspector, are you assuming a racial motive to this?'

'That's another possibility we have to consider,' she said coolly. 'The first victim was also a Pakistani businessman. Mr Rachid Aziz: do you know him?'

The least hesitation flickered across Younis's face. 'I – He is known to me, yes. We could not be described as friends.'

'And why's that?'

Asil Younis was plainly happier answering questions about his warehouse than about his relationship with Aziz. His tone hardened and he drew himself up tall. 'Isn't that rather presumptuous, Inspector, to suppose that because a man's parents were born in my part of the world we should necessarily be friends? Do you like every Englishwoman you meet? I think not. I have very little in common with Mr Aziz. He was a small shopkeeper; now he's not even that. I am, as you see, a successful businessman. He lives modestly, I do not. We are of a different generation: I was born in Pakistan, I believe Mr Aziz was born here in Castlemere. I know him to see, that is all. I do not understand why you expect there to be more.'

'There is more,' Liz insisted quietly. 'His empty shop was burned down on Friday night, your empty warehouse was burned down on Monday night.'

'And the Evans' thriving timberyard was burned down last night,' parried Younis. 'I also have no close ties with the Evans family. Perhaps you will find that easier to believe since my skin is not the same colour as theirs.'

Liz's first instinct was to deny the inference of that remark, her second to apologize. Sound instinct warned her that neither was necessary nor wise. She waited a moment, eyeing him speculatively, while her mind sieved out the nugget of information from that brief spat of invective. 'No close ties? Then you do at least know them, Mr Younis.'

It was obvious from everything he said, every inflection of his well-modulated faintly un-English voice and every unconscious gesture of his graceful hands, that Asil Younis was a supremely confident man, unaccustomed to the pangs of discomfiture which attend lesser mortals on a daily basis. But he was discomfited now, and it showed more because he was not used to it. 'Yes. No. I mean, of course I know them. They're members of the Chamber of Commerce, as I am. We use the same golf club. But it's not a personal acquaintance. You understand?'

Liz gave him a friendly uncomplicated smile to put him at his ease and still leave him wondering what she was thinking. 'Of course I understand, sir.' She thanked him for his time and left.

6

On his way to Superintendent Taylor's office Shapiro passed two men in the corridor. He barely glanced at them. Three paces further on he broke his stride and looked after them, puzzled at first and then remembering. 'Robin?'

Robin Taylor turned back with a ready smile on his handsome young face. 'Chief Inspector Shapiro. I didn't want to interrupt, you looked busy. It's good to see you.'

'Robin. Good grief. I haven't seen you since you were—' His hand hovered at about chest height.

The young man nodded. In fact he'd been eighteen the last time they met and already had Shapiro's bald spot in view, but he was too well mannered to say so.

'What are you doing with yourself now?' asked Shapiro.

'Same thing: the World Health Organization. I'm home for my sister's wedding, of course. It's a madhouse at home. I wish we were Catholics and could be sure once would be enough to keep her married for life.'

Shapiro chuckled. It was refreshing to speak to an intelligent, articulate, witty person under the age of thirty. Talking to David was like drawing teeth; talking to Donovan was like listening to rock music, you knew it was trying to tell you something but too many of the actual words made no sense. And if he overheard a conversation between detective constables it would concern either football or sex, and the depressing thing was how long he had to listen to be sure which.

'It could be worse,' he said. 'Women of the Nepalese hill tribes take several husbands at a time; often a family of brothers, to avoid dividing the farm.'

'Multiple bridegrooms – multiple best men,' mused Robin. 'Multiple rings to get lost. Multiple speeches containing amusing references to the stag night. Multiple humorous telegrams to be read out. Catholics or not, I think my mother will despatch Alison to a nunnery if the wedding arrangements get any more complicated than they are right now.' He turned then to include the other man in their conversation. 'Mr Shapiro, do you know my uncle? Major Ian Taylor of the Scots Guards.'

Major Taylor, a beefier version of his older brother with a moustache instead of a beard, seemed aware that Shapiro was pressed for time. He checked his watch, clapped the younger man on the shoulder. 'Come on, Robin, we have things to do and I'm sure the Chief Inspector has as well.'

'Glad to have met you,' said Shapiro. 'I'll see you at the wedding, no doubt.'

'If any of us stays sane that long,' chuckled Robin.

Shapiro continued on his way, equally cheered and depressed by the meeting. He was glad to see young Taylor looking fit and making something of his life. At the same time, it brought home what he couldn't help considering the mess David was making of his. There was less than a year between his son and the Taylor twins, and it was hard to believe that somewhere in the next nine months David too would begin to put down roots.

Superintendent Taylor was waiting for him, ushered him to a seat in a manner that immediately struck Shapiro as odd. James Taylor was a courteous man but they didn't usually play musical chairs.

Shapiro said, 'It's official now. Arson. Having a body makes it a murder inquiry.'

Taylor was watching from under lowered brows. 'The fire at the wharf?'

'Wasn't that what you wanted to see me about?'

'Actually, no.' The Superintendent chewed on the inside of his lip. 'This is going to be a bit of a shock, Frank, but something's come up that we have to talk about. Do you remember the Trevor Foot case?'

Shapiro retrieved it quickly from his mental database. It was eight years ago, soon after he came to this town, and the file was long ago closed by a successful conviction. But it had been an odd case, even briefly a celebrated one, and it still stood out from the background of burglaries and muggings that were the staple diet of Castlemere CID.

'Laboratory, wasn't it? That place out on The Levels – BioMedical Technology, they had a Home Office licence for animal experiments. What was the name of Foot's gang? – some bloody silly acronym. BEAST, that was it – Ban Experiments on Animals in Science Today.' His eyes kindled and his voice sharpened as recollection grew. 'That was arson, too. They razed the place to the ground, and a nightwatchman died. Is there a connection?'

'No – no,' Taylor said quickly. 'Frank, I hardly know how to say this so I'd better spit it out. There's been an allegation concerning that inquiry. That evidence was concealed in order to obtain Foot's conviction.'

Shapiro didn't know whether to laugh or cry. 'That's old news. Sir,' he added, reminding himself of Donovan's habit of rationing out courtesies like sips of water on a drifting lifeboat. 'Foot's whole defence was that I'd fitted him up. There was nothing else he could say: the evidence was against him, his brief had to discredit me if he was to put up any kind of a fight. He did his best, but the jury didn't believe him. They only retired out of politeness. For Heaven's sake, after eight years, why—?' His spread hand finished the question.

'I know.' Taylor's manner was apologetic. 'Frank, I *know* there's nothing in this. But you see my position. A serious allegation has been made, and now for the first time there appears to be some corroboration. I know—'

'*What* corroboration?' demanded Shapiro. 'There can't be.'

'Frank, please. I said there appeared to be. When we look into it I'm sure it'll be either a misunderstanding or bare-faced lies. Can you give me a little time to get it sorted out? A few days might do; a couple of weeks at most.

'With all the outcry these last few years over unsafe convictions I can't ignore it. We both know what I'll find: that the investigation was sound and any new information is either fabricated or so flimsy that nobody thought it worth introducing at the time. But, Frank, since we know that's going to be the outcome, better if you aren't here while I'm looking into it.'

Shapiro stared. 'You're suspending me?'

Taylor was quick to reassure him. 'Of course not. Frank, it's just a matter of form. We have to be seen to be accountable, that's all. I know a review of the case will vindicate your actions. But your position and mine will both be strengthened by the fact that a review took place.'

'You are.' Shock dulled Shapiro's voice. 'You're suspending me. Hell's bells, James, that's never happened to me before. Nobody ever said they didn't trust me to do my job.'

Taylor came quickly round the desk to him. 'Frank, nobody's saying that now. I have every confidence in you. But I have some obligations that are even higher than the loyalty I owe my best officers, and one is to be sensitive to public disquiet. Help me with this, please. You must be due some leave. You're always due leave. Take a fortnight now; when you get back it'll all be resolved. I promise you.'

'How can I?' Shapiro's gaze travelled round the office, suddenly less familiar than always, like a bird unsure if it was safe to alight. 'We're in the middle of an arson inquiry. One man's died already. God knows where this maniac'll

45

strike next, but with three fires in a week it won't be long and if he's graduated from derelict property there are going to be more casualties. How do I walk away from that?'

'You do it because I ask you to.' The Superintendent's tone was both gentle and firm. 'And because, if I have to, I'll insist. And you do it in the confidence that Inspector Graham will perform to the very best of her ability, and if she isn't quite in your league she's at least as good as anyone else we have or can get. She'll catch your arsonist, Frank, depend on it. And I'll lay this other matter to rest.'

Shapiro stood slowly, as if his limbs were numb and he couldn't feel the floor. He was stunned, like a man who's been in an accident. 'Er – what is this new evidence? You haven't told me.'

Taylor looked uneasy. 'I'm not sure I should, at least for now. It's important that you don't get involved.'

Indignation helped Shapiro get a grip on himself. 'What do you think I'm going to do, put the frighteners on Trevor Foot's old dad? Credit me with some intelligence. If you can't tell me who's produced this remarkable new evidence that changes the whole complexion of the case after eight years, fair enough. But I would like to know the nature of the allegation. I'm entitled to that, surely.'

After a moment Taylor nodded. 'Yes, I think you are. Someone's supposed to have spent the couple of days before the raid with Foot in London. The suggestion is that he couldn't have been involved in the BMT raid because he was with this person throughout the material time. There is a photograph that's supposed to prove it. The allegation is that you were given the original eight years ago and destroyed it because it cast doubt on your case against Foot.'

Shapiro was white; his voice actually shook. He knew the gravity of such a suggestion: if it wasn't disproved it would end his career. 'I never saw any photograph supporting Foot's defence. I sure as hell never destroyed any.'

'Of course not, they're just saying that to explain why it wasn't produced when it mattered. Don't worry about it. When we examine it it'll turn out to have been taken at some other time and that'll be the end of the matter.'

All the way back to his office Shapiro felt to be sleep-walking. Once he took a wrong turning. He literally bumped into Donovan who came out of the CID room with an unfolded copy of the *Castlemere Courier*.

'Sorry,' muttered Shapiro, continuing on his way.

'Sir?' Donovan's frown was puzzled. 'I've got something to show you.'

'Show Inspector Graham.'

'It's about the fires.'

'Inspector Graham'll deal with it.'

Most people would have taken the hint by then but Donovan pursued him along the corridor. 'Sir? She's not here, sir. And I've found something funny—'

Shapiro stopped. He sighed. 'Donovan, I don't care if you've found an unbroadcast edition of *The Goon Show*, it's no longer my concern. I'm going on holiday.'

Donovan couldn't have been more surprised if he'd said he was entering a monastery and his mail should be forwarded *via* Cardinal Hume. '*Now*, sir?'

'Now, Donovan.'

They'd reached the DCI's office. Shapiro tried to close the door between them but Donovan came in on his heels, the newspaper in his hand forgotten. There was a certain jerkiness to his movements, a terseness in his voice, that warned he was building up a head of steam.

'There's a man *dead* over this,' he said, as if Shapiro might need reminding. 'I grant you, Joey Banks wasn't much of a man. There wasn't a soul living would give you tuppence for him. He never had a job from the day he quit school to the day he died. For the last ten years home was whatever empty building or unlocked shed or stack of wood he could crawl into to keep the rain off, and he

47

lived on what he could beg, what he could steal and what he could find in dustbins.

'He was so nearly a non-person that even the people he drank with didn't know his real name. Bogle, they called him. Only some of his gear survived the fire: a Post Office book with three pounds in it and a letter from Social Services explaining why none of their benefits applied to him. Now, I know a man like that isn't worth much of anybody's time. Alive, he still wouldn't be. But Joey Banks is dead, murdered, and the man who killed him is wandering round out there with a cigarette lighter in his pocket, and – because of him if not because of Joey – I don't think this is the right time to be using up your holiday entitlement.'

For what came to feel like a long time Shapiro said nothing at all. He stepped round Donovan to close the door. He sat down behind his desk. He laid his hands palm down on its scuffed surface and studied his nails. Then he looked up and caught Donovan's angry, uncomprehending gaze in a grip of steel. 'One day, Sergeant,' he said softly, 'you will favour me with one of these paeans of righteous indignation, and the very next morning I will have you directing market traffic in Castle Square. I don't need to take this crap from you. From Superintendent Taylor I have to take it, but not from you.

'I'm going on leave, and I'm going now, because the only alternative I've been offered is suspension. Inspector Graham will take over the arson inquiry. She will, I have no doubt, be fascinated to learn what you've discovered in last week's *Courier*. She may even be interested in your opinion of me. But for the next ten or fifteen minutes, Sergeant Donovan, or however long it takes me to sort out a few things, this is still my office. And if you don't get out of it now, by God I'll throw you out.'

Donovan went then, the newspaper crumpled in his fist, his mind a maelstrom of questions. He thought for a moment, then went to the radio room. While he was

48

waiting for them to raise Liz Graham he tried to distil a little sense from the chaos in his head. But two quite trivial notions kept distracting him. One was that he'd never known Shapiro angry enough to say 'crap' before. And the other was that he'd no idea what a *Goon Show* was.

7

When Liz got the message she returned to Queen's Street at once. Donovan met her on the steps, told her the little he knew as they hurried upstairs. But Shapiro had already gone.

'Then I'll go see Taylor,' she said, tight lipped.

Casual acquaintances tended to think she was a nice woman and not go much further than that. Those who'd seen her working knew that the long fair hair, its curls subdued for business in a French pleat, the wide brow and the friendly green eyes concealed a core of adamant. She'd already reached a rank which made her rare in the essentially masculine world of criminal detection. Nice women don't do that.

But a superintendent outranks an inspector by two big steps and she didn't get the information she wanted. Taylor repeated what Donovan had already said, that Shapiro was taking leave while a matter arising from an earlier case was disposed of. In the meantime she was in charge of the arson inquiry.

'It's a murder inquiry now, sir. I'd understand if you wanted to bring in someone of a higher rank.'

Taylor smiled at her. He looked tired. 'What I want, Liz, is for Frank Shapiro to get back here as soon as possible and pick up where he left off. If I ask Scotland Yard for a visiting fireman, that's not going to happen. I know you haven't been here long, but I also know you're a good detective very much in Frank's own mould. If I

50

can't have him for a week or two I'm happy to have you instead. If you can tie it up in that time no one'll be more pleased than Frank. If not, you can wrap it up together after he gets back. All right?'

She was helpless to protest further. 'All right. This other matter: can I help with that?'

'Thank you, Inspector, but I'll handle it myself. Frank's got nothing to hide and I don't want it looking like a cover-up. You can help him best by assuring him that everything is under control and we're all looking out for his interests.' He gave a little secret smile into his beard. 'In the unlikely event, that is, of you seeing him.'

'It's right enough,' Liz said when she went back to Donovan. 'There's a complaint against him and he's on leave while it's dealt with. And I'm running the arson case.' She watched for his reaction.

Once in a blue moon Donovan said or did something of such generosity that it was possible for friends and colleagues to forgive the many tactless, abrupt and downright quarrelsome things he said and did in between. 'Well, thank Christ for that anyway. Listen, I've got something to show you.' He fetched his increasingly tatty copy of the *Castlemere Courier*.

'I was looking for a glazier.' He gave his saturnine smile. 'One who doesn't pale at the idea of windows that aren't square. And I found this.'

It was the timberyard's weekly advert. Liz read it carefully but couldn't see what he was getting at. 'So?'

He turned the page. 'Then I saw this.' It was the property column, commercial section. 'Investment opportunity – priced to allow for improvements – small shop off Milne Road, with vacant possession.'

'Rachid's Eight-Till-Late,' said Liz. 'We knew it was for sale.'

'By then I was curious,' said Donovan, 'so I kept looking. And on page three we find Councillor Morrison asking what's going to be done about all the empty property in the centre of Castlemere – everything from two-room flats in the Aldermaston Tower to a full-sized warehouse in Viaduct Lane.'

Liz gave a low whistle. 'You think our man's picking his targets out of the *Courier*?'

Donovan shrugged. 'I don't know. Two of them – the two adverts, say – I'd have taken as a coincidence. But all three? To me, that smells.'

Liz considered. 'Maybe it does, but does it help? We can't alert every business mentioned in last week's paper to the possibility of an arson attack. We'd have half the town in uproar. We have to narrow it down.'

'If he keeps this up for another week,' Donovan observed darkly, 'we can narrow it down to the places left standing.'

'What did you make of Rachid Aziz?'

'The guy's under pressure, the fire couldn't have come at a better time for him, but I doubt if he's the type. He knows Younis, though. Hasn't a good word to say for him.'

'It seems to be mutual. Younis said they had nothing in common, but I think it could be more personal than that.'

'Like, they've done a bit of business that now they're feeling vulnerable about?'

'It's possible, isn't it? I wouldn't put it past Younis to defraud his insurance. But then, why would he wait ten years?'

'And where does the timberyard fit in?'

'I can't see that it does. I was with the Evanses when I got your message, but I couldn't find a single reason any one of them would want the place to go up in smoke.'

'Maybe it's a red herring: whoever did the other two did the timberyard specifically to confuse us.'

Donovan inclined to the conspiracy theory of life. All the same, there was a kind of logic to it. He could be right. With three buildings in ashes and one man dead there was still so little to go on.

And nothing more they could usefully do that day. Except—

'I'm going to move into Mr Shapiro's office till he gets back. Give me a hand, will you?'

Donovan said nothing but his expression was eloquent. He didn't like it. He knew there were practical reasons for not leaving the DCI's office empty. If Shapiro had been sunning himself in the Mediterranean, or catching up on his decorating, or doing anything with leave taken in the normal way, he'd have had no qualms. But in the present circumstances it seemed too much like condoning what had been done. Donovan would rather have left the office empty, a constant reproach.

When they'd finished Liz said, 'It won't be for long. We'll be doing this again before the dust's settled.'

'Yes, ma'am.'

It had taken blood, sweat and tears to get him to use her proper title the first time: now she ground her teeth over it, taking it – as he meant it – as censure bordering on insult. 'Go home, Donovan,' she said wearily. 'Get your windows fixed.'

Shapiro was drinking. It wasn't something he did much, he didn't like it enough. But his head hurt with trying to remember where he'd gone wrong with the Foot case, how he'd left himself open to an accusation that eight years later his superintendent had no choice but to act on. And for the life of him he couldn't. So he drank.

When the doorbell rang, his first thought was that he'd had one Scotch too many and the noise was in his head. Then it rang again, so probably he hadn't imagined it. After a little while he got up and opened it.

David stood at an angle on the doorstep, as if half ready to leave. His hair was tousled and his clothes smelled of smoke. 'Dad.'

'Ha!' said Shapiro, obscurely, sending a blast of Scotch fumes into the night.

Slowly, incredulously, David began to smile. 'You're drunk.'

'I have drink taken,' Shapiro amended pontifically. 'It

53

is possible I would not pass a breathalyser.'

'You're drunk.'

'I am tired and emotional.'

'As a newt,' chuckled David. 'Can I come in?'

He hadn't seen the house before. After his marriage broke up Shapiro sold the family home and moved into this stone cottage at the foot of Castle Mount. It was more than enough for a man on his own.

'It's nice,' said David. 'Does it have a spare room?'

Shapiro squinted at him. 'I thought you were staying with Donovan.'

'I'm in the way there now. There's really only the saloon that's habitable.' His sharp jaw came up. 'Of course, if it's any trouble—'

'No trouble,' Shapiro said hastily, 'no trouble. Spare room's' – he indicated the stairs – 'up there somewhere.'

David smiled. 'I'll find it.'

Shapiro was certainly drunk but not insensible. As David started up the stairs he said, 'Donovan told you, didn't he? About my problems.'

And David was a poor liar. He said, 'No, he didn't,' when he should have said, 'What problems?'

Shapiro smiled into the chest of his cardigan. 'Go find your room.'

When David returned there was coffee steaming on the kitchen table. Shapiro had already made a start on it and sobriety loomed. David sat down. 'Is it serious?'

Shapiro laughed but no sound came out. 'Oh no, it's the sort of thing that happens every day. Somebody says you lied in order to jail an innocent man and your superior officer won't take your word that you didn't. And he won't trust you not to interfere in his investigation so he tells you to go home until he's decided whether his chief of detectives or a convicted criminal is more likely to be telling the truth. An everyday tale of provincial policing, that.'

'I suppose,' ventured David, 'this is the price we pay

54

for accountability. In order to be sure nobody's playing the system they have to be willing to look at anyone who might be.'

'Well, thank you for that in-depth analysis,' Shapiro said nastily. It was partly the drink, but he wouldn't have spoken to his newest police cadet that way. He sighed. 'I know about accountability; I *approve* of accountability. Without Complaints Investigation a senior police officer has the sort of power over people's lives that ships' captains used to have: master under God. The good ones can make a mistake. The bad ones have scope for real corruption. I accept that allegations have to be investigated.

'But David, it *hurts*. Never mind the principles, never mind the need for safeguards: when somebody says that an innocent man's been in prison for eight years because I fitted him up, that hurts. Do you understand? It's a real physical pain, like a knife under my ribs. It's as if nothing I've done in the eight years since has any validity, because the people who know me best think I could have done that.'

'But you didn't, did you?' It was more a statement than a question.

'No, of course not. I don't understand. Taylor said there were some photographs, but we never saw any photographs. It was an open-and-shut case. A laboratory was fire-bombed, some animal fanatics claimed responsibility, Trevor Foot was heard boasting about it in a pub and we picked him up. He didn't even deny it, he just played games with us. He had a history of joining extremist groups and he had connections with this one. Also, he'd been missing from his work for two days before the raid. Sure, when it went to court he said he'd been framed. But he wasn't. For one thing there was no need. He admitted what he'd done in front of witnesses because he was daft enough to be proud of it. The jury were hardly out long enough to elect a foreman and take a vote. They knew he was guilty.'

'Then you've nothing to worry about.'

'I'm not worried,' Shapiro snapped. 'I'm – angry.'

'Every day,' said David quietly, 'the police question people about crimes they didn't commit. When that becomes obvious they're released, with an apology if they're lucky. That's the position you're in. Next time you find you've picked up the wrong guy, remember how it feels.'

As Shapiro regarded his son through the clearing mists of alcohol his brow furrowed. They'd always had arguments. For years at a time they'd hardly spoken except in anger. He wasn't sure how it began, though in his fairer moments he knew better than to blame a child for a breakdown in communications with an adult.

David was the last of his children and the least like him. Rachael was as tall as her father, had the same broad face and fought – as he had given up fighting – the same tendency to stoutness. Sally looked like her mother but thought like him. But there was no explaining David: nothing of either himself or Angela about the boy, in appearance or any other way.

Angela was a tall slender woman with, in her youth, hair the colour of a wheatfield streaked with poppies. Shapiro was of average height with curves where most young men have angles. He was never quick enough for a policeman: he tried hard but he wasn't designed for speed. Fortunately his promotions came rapidly and he soon found himself in jobs where intellect mattered more than fitness. Once he made Detective Sergeant his colleagues stopped running sweepstakes on how many criminals would outstrip him each month, how old they might be and whether any of them would have wooden legs, and started noticing how many convictions he got in other ways.

So Frank Shapiro was the last man to expect perfection of his children. He loved Rachael with her broad sunny face, who from the age of three looked like the teacher she would become; and he loved Sally with her swift mind and sharp tongue, and the river of golden hair she tossed over her shoulder to end any argument she was in danger of losing. He expected Sally to become an actress, was startled to find himself the proud father of a civil engineer.

Loving his son was harder. The small dark intense child seemed to need things the girls had not, which Shapiro could not identify, much less provide. There was no joy in him. He did well at school but flayed himself in the process. He was a talented musician but took no pleasure in music, made of it only another rod for his back.

Angela understood better than Shapiro. 'He needs your approval, Frank. Tell him you're proud of him.'

Shapiro was astonished. 'I do. All the time.'

'No, you don't. You praise what he's done. Top of the class – well done, David. The music prize – congratulations, David, knew you had it in you. He thinks he has to do things to please you. The trouble with that is, if he wins the music prize this year, what's he going to have to do next year?'

Shapiro had huffed and snorted about that, pretended not to know what she was saying. Later, alone, he thought about it and found that he did understand. But he didn't know what to do about it. Frank Shapiro and his son lacked the vocabulary to discuss anything that mattered. There was something brittle and impervious about the boy that shrugged off efforts to reach him. Shapiro hadn't felt a failure since he was last outrun by a geriatric shoplifter, but his son made him feel a failure.

If the Shapiros had had friends with children, so that he could have leaned on bars and exchanged horror stories with other fathers of growing sons, Frank would have found there was nothing unusual about his problems. Teenage boys are full of paradox, the despair of fathers throughout the land. If Shapiro had known that it would have been easier for both of them.

But by the time David was growing up Shapiro's career

had taken him past the point of sharing personal confidences with colleagues and he had no close friends outside work. He believed his failure with his son was something unique to them, and he regretted it but never found a way past it. When Angela decided that twenty-four years was long enough to live with a policeman, David left with her. A year later he was studying photography in Brighton. Shapiro could count on the fingers of one hand the number of times he'd seen him since.

Now they were arguing again, but there was a difference. David had become a man, had learned somewhere the confidence in his own opinions that he should have got from his father, and Shapiro felt a sudden respect for him. After all this time. He still looked like a drop-out. He was still wasting his energies on what seemed to Shapiro more like a hobby than a job. But in the years of separation two things had happened. David had grown up, and Shapiro had let go.

He was still bemused but no longer affronted by the choices David had made. He no longer felt responsible for his son's shortcomings. For the first time it was possible for them to meet a little like strangers, and to base their judgements of each other on what they saw instead of what they remembered. Time had built up a burden of anger, and more time had laid it to rest.

Shapiro said quietly, 'I'm glad you're here.' David only flicked him a tiny fleeting smile and poured more coffee. 'How long can you stay?'

David explained about Payne and the badgers. 'I'll give him till the weekend, then I'm going back to London. I can't afford to waste any more time on this.'

'You got your fire pictures, though,' said Shapiro. 'Are you pleased with them?'

David looked at him in surprise. Another first: his father showing an interest in his work. 'Yes, I am. They'd have been better if I could have got inside, though.'

'Where did you develop them?'

58

'The *Courier* lent me their darkroom in return for first refusal on the prints. They're taking a couple of them: at least I shan't be out of pocket on the week.'

'Stick around a bit longer,' suggested Shapiro grimly, 'we might manage another one. This chap's still on the loose, and I'm damned if I know how to find him. If it was still my job, which it isn't.' He brightened. 'You could come to Alison Taylor's wedding with me next Tuesday. Weren't you at school with the Taylor kids?'

'Batman and the Vestal Virgin? Sure.'

Shapiro laughed out loud. 'Why did you call them that?'

David shrugged. 'Batman, Robin – you know. Anyway it suited him. Alison's all right. The only problem with her was her dad. When she was seventeen he still wanted her home by nine o'clock.'

Shapiro sighed. 'You worry about girls. I used to worry about Sally. Rachael was always terribly competent, from about fourteen she worried about me, but there was something vulnerable about Sally.'

'Sally,' David said firmly, 'is and always was about as vulnerable as an armadillo.'

After a long pause, afraid of breaking something, Shapiro said, 'I worried about you too.'

David's expression tightened. 'I made out all right.'

'I know. But I should have done better by you. I don't know why, I always felt – out of my depth.'

If only David could have met him halfway then. If he'd smiled and said, 'We both made mistakes.' If he'd made a joke about it: 'The first twenty years are the worst.' But he didn't. His eyes low, he just said again, 'I made out.'

They hardly said anything more until they went to bed.

8

If Aziz and Younis had been a couple of Irishmen, Donovan would have spent an evening in the Fen Tiger, where Castlemere's small Irish community congregated. He'd have bought a few drinks, started a few conversations, and by chucking-out time would have had some idea of the relationship between the two men, whether they were likely to have concocted something like an insurance fraud and then fallen out over it.

But the Pakistanis were Moslems and if they drank it wasn't in public, and Donovan couldn't think where else casual acquaintances might be persuaded to talk about them. The only place he knew they had mutual friends was the mosque and he doubted his ability to engage anyone there in gossip.

Then he thought of the school. Both men had raised children in the town, they had to be educated somewhere: Younis could have afforded private schools but he might have considered it more important for his sons to grow up in the town where they were going to do business. As local businessmen both would have been parent-governor material, and if they'd served on a school committee together he could talk to the people who'd served with them.

Castlemere had more than one secondary school but Castle High was the likeliest choice. Of the alternatives, one essentially served the big housing estate on the edge of town where neither family lived; one was called St

Elwyn's, which while open to all wouldn't appeal to non-Christian families; and one prided itself on its aggressively modern approach. Both Younis and Aziz seemed like men who would prefer examination results to creative self-expression.

Also, Donovan knew someone who taught at Castle High.

Brian Graham, called out of his Thursday morning history of art class, greeted Donovan cautiously. 'Did Liz send you?' He had nothing against the detective, beyond a few sleepless nights while his wife sat up fuming about him, but he liked order and being around Donovan was like handling a live grenade.

'Not really.' Donovan gave his vulpine grin. 'I'm showing my initiative.'

When he explained what he wanted Graham took him to the school secretary who produced the enrolment list. 'Yes, we have an Aziz – Nazreen Aziz, aged fourteen, parents Mr and Mrs Rachid Aziz, Rosedale Road. Is that the right one?'

Donovan nodded. 'How about Younis?'

She hadn't a current Younis but tracked down two ex-pupils. 'Salman and Fakhar Younis – parents Mr and Mrs Asil Younis, Cambridge Road?'

'Bingo,' said Donovan. 'Were Mr Younis and Mr Aziz ever on the school board together?'

The woman took the disc out of her computer with a sniff, put in a different one. 'If you'd asked me that to start with, Sergeant, we could have saved ourselves some time.' She keyed up a display. 'No. Mr Younis was a parent-governor for six years, until two years ago when his younger son went up to Reading. Mr Aziz has never served on the school board.'

'Oh,' said Donovan, disappointed. 'Well – their kids weren't in the same class and they wouldn't have played the same sports. Anything else they might have done together?' He was thinking of music or dramatic societies,

61

something that might have meant the two fathers meeting after rehearsals or at concerts.

The secretary looked at him suspiciously. 'Are you sure you've got the authority for this?'

'What authority do I need?' he asked, surprised. 'Isn't it a matter of public record who serves on a school board?'

'Well, yes, probably,' she admitted. 'But I'm not going to call up the children's files without a direct instruction from the principal.'

Until then Donovan hadn't considered that the connection might be the children themselves. But Younis had sons and Aziz had daughters, so he considered it now. 'Then I'd better talk to the principal.'

'You did *what*?' demanded Inspector Graham, her eyes great with despair. 'And you involved my husband in this?'

'He wasn't involved. He showed me the way to the secretary's office, and she showed me to the principal's office,' said Donovan. 'And the principal said that pupil files were strictly confidential and I'd need a warrant to see them. And then she said that, so far as she knew, all that was in the past anyway.'

Liz frowned. 'All what?'

'Well, exactly,' said Donovan. 'All whatever it was that was in those files I couldn't see. So I wondered what you wanted me to do next. Do we have grounds for a warrant?'

Liz didn't even have to think. 'Not at this stage. We've no convincing reason to suspect Aziz and Younis, we can't investigate their families until we have.'

'So I guess waylaying Nazreen Aziz at the school gates and asking her what she was up to with the Younis boys is out of the question too, huh?'

She didn't think he was serious, but just in case she spelled it out. 'Absolutely out of the question, Sergeant.'

'I could try Aziz again, ask him why he didn't tell me

62

his daughter was friendly with Younis's son.'

'It may not have been that they were friends.'

'In that case he'll tell me what it was instead. He led me to believe there was no connection between himself and Younis, but there's something. I think maybe if he knows I know that much, he'll tell me the rest.'

Liz nodded slowly. 'All right. But go gently with him. It could be a touchy subject, and it's still an outside chance that he's done anything wrong. Try not to upset him for no good reason.'

'Me, boss?' Donovan wasn't very good at injured innocence but that didn't stop him trying. 'I'm the soul of discretion, me.'

'Yes,' said Liz heavily. 'And I'm the Dalai Lama.'

Rachid Aziz was surprised to see Donovan again, annoyed at being approached at the supermarket where he worked. Neither made him seem like a man with a serious crime to hide.

'I asked your supervisor, he'd no objections,' said Donovan. 'He assumed it was something to do with your fire.'

Aziz blinked. 'Isn't it?'

'You tell me.'

They found a little privacy walking through the unloading bay. Donovan said carefully, 'When I asked if you knew Asil Younis, you said he wasn't a man you'd want your family associating with. You didn't tell me about your daughter and his son.'

The conversation skipped a beat. Then Aziz said, a shade faintly, 'My daughter?'

'Your daughter Nazreen. His son Fakhar.' It was a bit of a gamble on Donovan's part. But Aziz's younger daughter was still at primary school and Younis's elder son would have left Castle High before Nazreen got there. Even Fakhar was five years her senior, their time at Castle High overlapping by only a couple of years.

Rachid Aziz was not a big man but he drew himself up

63

like one. 'This is a family matter. You have no right.'

'Your fire was one of a series in which a man died,' Donovan reminded him. 'That gives me the right.'

Aziz accepted that. His voice dropped. 'But this is a matter affecting my daughter's honour.'

Some people might have found that laughable. But Donovan wasn't as much of a cynic as he made out and actually was rather touched. 'Then let's deal with it now, between us, once and for all.'

Aziz saw sense in that, but it still took him a moment to find the words. 'My daughter Nazreen attracted the attention of a much older boy at her school. Fakhar Younis was already sixteen years old when she went to Castle High at the age of eleven. This is not perhaps so unusual among our people, but it was not something I wished to encourage. I thought when he went to university that would be the end of it.

'But he kept in touch with her, and it is fair to say that his attentions were not unwelcome to Nazreen. The next thing I knew I had Mr Younis on my doorstep wishing to contract a formal engagement between them. Nazreen was then fourteen years old.

'I told him I would not countenance such a thing, that if Nazreen and Fakhar wished to marry when she was eighteen I would not withhold my consent but that I considered it altogether too soon to be making long-term plans for so young a child. And he said to me' – Aziz flushed with anger, the colour plain through the olive of his skin – 'he said, "But in four years' time she might not be a virgin." '

'You must have found that very offensive,' Donovan said quietly.

The glance Aziz cast him was almost grateful. 'I did. Oh, I know it is fashionable in this country to say that virginity does not matter, only being careful. That it is natural and inevitable for young people to experiment with sex, and as long as there are no babies and no disease that is all right and anyway parents can do more harm than good by condemning it.

'Well, perhaps that is so in the English community. I do not know. I live in an Asian community, and to us purity is important. Our children are not promiscuous. My wife and I were both pure at our marriage in our early twenties; and we didn't have to be signed away in a contract of engagement at the age of fourteen to ensure it. Mr Younis suggested that my daughter was a slut, and that I was a bad father who could not take care of her until she was old enough to contemplate marriage. Indeed, I found that most offensive.'

'So you told him where to go?'

Aziz hung his head. 'I regret to say, Sergeant Donovan, that I struck him.'

Donovan preserved a straight face. 'So if he was looking for someone to share in a dodgy enterprise, someone who either respected or feared him enough to do as he was told when the going got tough, someone who could be relied on to care more for his financial situation than his honour, yours probably wouldn't be the first name to spring to mind.'

Aziz understood what he was saying. He smiled ruefully. 'I do not believe so, no.'

'Perhaps we'd better look somewhere else for our firebug.'

'It might have been Mr Younis on his own,' said Aziz hopefully, and they both chuckled. Then he said, 'I'm sure you understand, Sergeant, that what I have told you should remain in confidence if at all possible. For my daughter's sake.'

'No problem,' said Donovan. 'It has no bearing on the case we're investigating. I don't expect to have to talk to you about it again, let alone to anyone else.'

'You know what you've done now, don't you?' Liz said wearily. 'You've dug a hole under our only theory.'

'I've succeeded in disproving an erroneous theory, ma'am, yes,' said Donovan with dignity. 'Isn't it you's always telling me police work is not about getting convictions, it's about establishing truth?'

'It was your theory in the first place.'

'Indeed it was, ma'am. Anybody'd think I was the only one in this place doing any work.'

'Get out of here!' She aimed a rolled-up newspaper at him but he dodged round her door before she could throw it.

David was out and Shapiro was wallowing in a hot bath when the phone rang. His immediate reaction was to let it ring. He wasn't on duty. He wasn't on call. He was on holiday. But the habits of thirty years go deep, and after listening to it with mounting irritation for perhaps a minute he got out of the bath and padded dripping into the bedroom to answer it. 'This had better be good.'

'Mr Shapiro?' It was a woman's voice. 'It's Gail Fisher, at the *Courier*. I'm sorry to bother you at home, Chief Inspector, but I tried your office and they said you wouldn't be in for a day or two. We're about to go to press and I wanted to give you the chance to comment on this Foot business.'

Shapiro's heart sank. Perhaps it had been too much to hope that the paper wouldn't get hold of it, that the inquiry could be held and his performance vindicated without the matter leaving Queen's Street. There were other people involved: Foot for one, this witness who claimed to have been with him for another. Somebody must have thought that the oxygen of publicity would breathe fresh life into their cause.

'I'm sorry, Miss Fisher, there's nothing I can say about it. Allegations have been made which are being investigated by my superiors. When they reach a conclusion I'll be informed. I dare say you'll hear too.' He hadn't meant that as sourly as it sounded.

'When you're vindicated it'll give me the greatest possible pleasure to say so, in the largest print I can find.'

Shapiro appreciated her confidence. 'I'll look forward to that.' He paused, a certain diffidence creeping in. 'Um – would it be terribly unprofessional for me to ask what you'll be saying this week?'

'Just that the case has been reopened,' Fisher said. 'And a résumé of the original facts and findings. That's about all; unless you want to go on record as denying a cover-up.'

Shapiro scowled. 'So you heard that too. You wouldn't by any chance have seen these photographs as well?'

He could hear her grin. 'Not yet.'

'Well, that makes two of us,' he said heavily. 'And you can quote me on that.' He thought for a moment, steaming gently. 'Where did you pick this up? It's still internal at this stage.'

There was the briefest of pauses, as if he'd surprised her. 'You don't know?'

'If I knew,' he said patiently, 'I wouldn't have to ask.'

There was another, longer hiatus. 'Chief Inspector, you're putting me in a difficult position. I can't tell you where I first heard the case was being reopened.'

'You have a source to protect? Who? This witness who claims to have been with Foot while someone else was bombing BMT? The one with the photographs?'

'No,' she said, firmly enough that it was probably true. 'No, I don't know who that is. Yet. I'll be trying to find out.'

'Who, then? Foot himself? He's been claiming I framed him for eight years, why would you suddenly listen to him now?'

'Chief Inspector—'

'It had to be Foot. Apart from him and his brief, and this star witness of theirs, the only people who know what's going on work in my office.'

'Mr Shapiro, I'm sorry if I seem evasive. I'm confused.

I thought you knew where the story came from. I thought it had your blessing.'

'My *blessing*? Whyever would you think that?'

'Because it really didn't come from Trevor Foot, Chief, that's why.'

9

When he finished work on Thursday evening, labouring
by torchlight because his power cable was buried under
the remains of a wall, Donovan began shovelling rubble
and broken glass out of the wreckage of his home into
sacks that he then lugged up on to the tow-path. He'd
found a glazier who was going to call the next day: now
he had to clear enough debris for the man to reach the
windows.

After three hours he'd had enough. The job wasn't
finished but he'd broken its back; if he did much more
tonight he thought he'd break his own. In the galley he
set water to heat on the gas stove: half for the coffee pot,
half for a wash.

When *Tara* eased fractionally to the weight of someone
stepping aboard he stopped and listened, expecting to be
hailed. But no one called so he wiped the soap out of his
eyes with a rag of towel and pushed the hatch open.
'Who's there?'

'It's me.' But Shapiro, normally the most courteous of
men, didn't wait for an invitation before descending the
companionway with the heavy caution of someone who
considered living on a boat both unnatural and perverse.

'Chief?' Even in one word Donovan couldn't mask his
surprise. 'Come in, sit down – if you can find anywhere
clean. Watch your step, there's a lot of rubbish about still.'

Shapiro took the torch off the galley table and shone
it ahead of him. 'You should have got David to give you

a hand.' His voice was flat, expressionless. He wasn't here to discuss Donovan's domestic crisis. It wasn't any kind of a social call.

Donovan dried himself roughly, groped for his shirt. 'I'm better working on my own.' He dared a grin that the darkness kept Shapiro from seeing. 'You may have noticed this.'

The torch swung round, blinding him. He put up a hand to shield his eyes but Shapiro kept the light full on his face. His voice tight with anger he demanded, 'Whatever possessed you, going to the papers?'

Donovan squinted into the light, trying to see past it. 'What do you mean? I don't know what you're talking about.'

Shapiro's laugh was bitter and ironic. 'Don't give me that just-off-a-potato-boat routine, Sergeant, I've seen it before. You're not some dumb Paddy, though dear God, often enough you act like one. But you're not getting a fool's pardon this time.'

Donovan too was growing angry. He didn't think he deserved this, and even if he did Shapiro owed it to him to explain how. He growled, 'Get that damned light out of my eyes and tell me what it is I'm supposed to have done, 'cause I haven't the foggiest notion what you're doing here. Sir.' He always thought he could get away with murder if he said 'sir' at the end.

'Gail Fisher called me. From the *Courier*.'

'Did she?'

'She wanted to know if I'd care to comment on the reopening of the Foot case.'

'So?'

Shapiro was breathing heavily in the darkness behind the torch. 'So how did she know the Foot case was being reopened, Sergeant?'

It was a powerful torch, the strongest he had, and Donovan still couldn't look at it without flinching. It made him look as if he had something to hide. Provoked beyond his admittedly meagre fund of patience he struck out, batting the beam aside. 'What are you saying? That she got it from me?'

'The last time I saw you,' gritted Shapiro, 'you were waving a copy of the *Courier* under my nose. And she as good as told me it was someone in my office gave her the story.'

'I don't care what she told you,' Donovan said forcefully, 'and I don't care how it looks. I didn't tell Gail Fisher or anyone else at the *Courier* about the Foot case. I didn't tell anyone who could have told anyone at the *Courier*. I don't gossip about our business. Or anything else, as it happens.'

The trouble was, Shapiro believed him. If he hadn't been so angry he'd have known it was a non-starter: Donovan was so disinclined to gossip that getting routine information out of him was like drawing teeth. Another man, well meaning but not necessarily a great thinker, might have decided the publicity would help. But that wasn't Donovan's style either. If he'd felt strongly enough about it – and taking virtues, such as loyalty, to the kind of extremes where they become vices such as obstinacy was his speciality – he'd have raised it with Superintendent Taylor not a reporter.

Anger had kept him going: robbed of it Shapiro suddenly felt old and tired. He sighed, put down the torch. 'No. I'm sorry, Donovan, I know you better than that. I think maybe it's as well I'm – on holiday. I'm really not thinking very straight about all this, am I?'

The Irish are a sentimental people and Donovan was a sucker for pathos. He brushed debris off a galley stool, heedless of the shards of glass pricking his hands. 'Sit down, Chief. Tell me what's happened. Tell me how I can help.'

The first task was easier than the second. 'Top and bottom of it is, lad, you can't help. It's up to God now.' The backwash from the torch showed doubt in Donovan's narrow face and Shapiro smiled faintly. 'Superintendent Taylor to you.'

Donovan was too troubled to be amused. 'Why would anyone from Queen's Street go to the papers? There's nobody there believes for a minute that you fitted Foot up.'

Shapiro shrugged. 'I thought maybe someone wanted the *Courier* to take up cudgels on my behalf. Someone with my interests at heart but a gale whistling between his ears.'

'So you naturally thought of me.'

'I have apologized for that,' Shapiro said with dignity. 'Er – what was it in the paper that you wanted to show me?'

Donovan told him. He saw Shapiro's interest quicken, then subside again. 'Well, that's none of my business now. I expect Inspector Graham will get to the bottom of it.'

'Yeah,' said Donovan.

'Yes,' said Shapiro thoughtfully.

Liz and Brian had been in bed for half an hour when Brian's sinuses started itching and he thought he'd open the window another notch. But he went on standing at the drawn curtain until Liz looked up and said, 'What is it?'

'I'm not sure,' he said, bewildered. 'But I think it's Frank Shapiro's car parked across our drive.'

She wrapped a dressing-gown round her T-shirt, slid her feet into slippers and went to see why.

Shapiro had been sitting there for twenty minutes, unable to decide whether to ring the bell or go home. When the hall light came on he fumbled for the ignition; then she was padding towards him and he couldn't for shame cut and run, spitting gravel at her from under his wheels. He wound his window down.

'Frank, for Heaven's sake come inside.'

'No,' he said. 'I only—'

'Come inside.

72

Her hair fell in a long loose plait down her back. He'd never seen it down, hadn't realized there was so much of it. Pulled out straight it would be as long as Sally's. My God, he thought in sudden despair, what are you *doing*? You're waxing lyrical about a detective inspector's *hair*!

She was making coffee and so didn't witness his confusion. When it was done she turned back with a smile. 'Now then, what's going on?'

It was too late in the day to do anything else so he told her the truth. 'I wondered if you knew anything about it.'

'You wondered if I told the *Courier* that you'd been sent on holiday while your conduct of an eight-year-old case was being investigated?'

'No,' he said. 'No. Well, maybe a little bit.'

'Why me?'

'I've already seen Donovan.'

She laughed but there was an edge to it. 'I bet he was thrilled.'

'I thought he was going to hit me,' admitted Shapiro.

She watched him over the top of her mug. 'I haven't spoken to Gail Fisher or anyone else about this.'

'I know that.' His eyes were downcast, his whole demeanour apologetic. 'Oh, God, Liz, I'm doing this so badly. Not just' – he waved a shaky hand round her kitchen – 'this whole business. Being suspended. Because that's what it is, whatever Taylor chooses to call it. I hate it and I can't handle it. I don't think I could feel any worse about it if I'd done what I'm supposed to have and the skeletons were queuing up to fall out of the cupboard.'

'But there aren't any. Skeletons, I mean.'

'None that I know of. As far as I know, that investigation was copybook. I don't care who looks at it or how strong the magnifying glass, they won't find irregularities.'

Liz smiled. 'Then there's nothing to worry about.'

'Except which of my officers is giving confidential press briefings and claiming it's with my approval.' His voice was rough.

'She didn't exactly say that though, did she? You don't think maybe it was a misunderstanding? That in trying not to say where she heard the story she inadvertently gave you the idea it came from Queen's Street? I just don't believe it. Nobody we work with would go behind your back like that.'

He wanted so much to believe she was right. Unconvincingly he shrugged it off. 'Oh, what the hell. There's no real harm done. Perhaps it's better out in the open, then when it's finished with everybody'll know.' He made a determined effort to put it out of his mind. 'Any progress with your fires?'

Liz shook her head. 'None. It's one step forward and two steps back. Donovan's conspiracy theory came to nothing: there is a connection between Younis and Aziz but it's not friendship, it's bad blood – they don't trust one another enough to do something dodgy together. And I don't have any other leads.'

'What about an Old Boys' Reunion?' She didn't understand. 'Haul in anyone you can find with form for this kind of thing and sweat them, see who coughs.' He heard himself talking like Donovan and winced. 'Even if nobody admits it you might learn something from the trade gossip.'

'How many ex-arsonists do we have in Castlemere?'

'Offhand I can think of' – Shapiro sniffed and gave the light fitting a deliberate look – 'well, none actually. Unless you count John Ho at the Golden Dragon, to whom the combustion point of fried rice remains one of the mysteries of the Orient.'

In spite of the gravity of the matter Liz chuckled. 'So no Old Boys' Reunion. Then what do I do instead? Help me, Frank, I'm out of my depth here.'

He shook his head wearily. 'We're all out of our depth when it comes to something like this. You do what you can think of and hope to get lucky. In the end he's as likely to be caught by a beat copper curious about a late-night walker with no dog as by clever detective work.'

'I can't just sit on my hands and wait for fortune to smile! One man's already died: God knows how many more people will be hurt or killed if we don't wrap this up soon.'

'What about the fuel? Whatever he uses, he must be getting through a good bit of it. Unless he's bright enough to use petrol siphoned out of his car, he's probably buying it by the can somewhere. Probably somewhere different each time. Since he won't want to walk home carrying a petrol can with every fire appliance in Castlemere coming towards him, he'll use it up and dump it each time. So he's probably bought a can of petrol, or maybe paraffin, from three different suppliers in the last fortnight. You could ask around the garages and hardware shops, see if anyone they didn't know has asked for fuel in a can over the last couple of weeks.

'Another thing: what happened to the cans? Like I say, he wouldn't want to be found in possession – particularly if, like most arsonists, he likes standing in the crowd watching the Fire Brigade at work. Bit of a give-away, standing there with your can smelling of petrol. So he gets rid of it. Silcott would have said if his people had found it in the debris but check anyway.

'If he didn't leave it behind, it may be he was afraid it could be traced to him. So he dumped it somewhere else. But it had to be somewhere handy, and somewhere either it wouldn't be found or it wouldn't be noticed. You could have a diver search the canal at the back of the timber-yard. See if there's a dump or a builder's skip or anything near the shop and the warehouse. And check with the nearest garage in each case: the best place to hide a brick's in a wall.'

Liz groaned, appalled by the scale of the task. 'Even if we find it, what's it going to tell us? He'll hardly have left his fingerprints all over it.'

'You never know your luck,' said Shapiro. 'But even

without prints it may tell you something. Particularly if you find all three. If you can discover where they were bought they'll tell you something about his movements. They may have collected dust and grease from his garage in which case they'll be a positive forensic link when you do find him. They may – oh, I don't know, but I think you ought to find them if you can.'

'All right, I'll get on to it first thing tomorrow.' She hesitated before continuing. 'Look, I know you're on holiday, and I know you have to keep away from the Foot business, but would you mind if I kept in touch over this? To be honest I don't know that I've got the experience to handle it. I'd feel better if I could just talk to you from time to time.'

It was as pretty a compliment as Frank Shapiro could remember. 'Any time. Phone me or come round, any time. But trust your own instincts too. Taylor wouldn't have you running this if he didn't think you were up to it, and I think so too. Listen.' He hauled himself to his feet and headed for the door. 'About the other thing. I'm sorry. I'm sorry for thinking it, sorry for saying it and sorry for disturbing you at this time of night. Tell Brian I'm sorry, will you?'

'If he's still awake.'

Shapiro was too tired to drive. The trouble with driving when you're tired is that things happen faster than your mind can deal with them so that accidents happen. He was also too tired to think. The trouble with thinking when you're tired is that your mind works too quickly and runs out of control, and you haven't the concentration to discriminate between good thinking and bad. That's why minor problems seem insuperable during the night, crazy ideas seem brilliant, and things that you don't want to think about at all force themselves into your head.

They battle their way to the surface of your brain and lay siege to you, and pound away at you until in sheer exhaustion you give way and consider them. That's what happened to Shapiro on his drive home. In the daytime he might have had the same idea but dismissed it before it was more than a bad taste in his mouth. But because it was late and he was tired he let it into his head where it took root, and soon he was considering something he very much didn't want to.

David was in bed when he got home, catching up on lost sleep. If Shapiro had had the sense to wait until morning it wouldn't have seemed so important to either of them. But he'd already made a fool of himself with his colleagues and he wanted retribution for that as well. He clumped up to the spare room and turned the light on, and waited stony-faced while the boy blinked awake.

'Wha— what's the matter?'

'Tell me again about your arrangement with the *Courier*,' Shapiro said coldly.

II

1

The *Castlemere Courier* was printed on Thursday evening and on sale from Friday morning. It enjoyed a healthy local circulation since it made a point of carrying the news readers were genuinely interested in – bowling league results, who'd been in court for drunken driving and which borough councillors had made idiots of themselves at this month's meeting – rather than merely important matters like foreign wars and whether the government would survive another economic scandal.

But the *Courier* had rarely been scanned with such intensity as it was this Friday morning in the CID offices at Queen's Street. There was so much in it that concerned them.

There were accounts of all three fires. The first, at Rachid's the previous Friday, had come at that nightmare time for a weekly newspaper, too late to carry the story that week and old as the hills by the next. There were pictures too: the ashes of the first two, more spectacular shots of the timberyard fire at its height with David Shapiro's by-line prominently displayed.

There was a paragraph on the reopening of the Foot inquiry. As Shapiro had hoped it was brief and to the point: the police were looking into the possibility that fresh evidence had become available. Nothing in the wording or slant of the report indicated its origins.

Then there was the chance that the paper was being used as a menu, and that any property mentioned in any

81

context – advertising columns, news reports, forthcoming events, anything at all – was fair game for a pyromaniac. So for perhaps half an hour after the papers came in there was no sound to be heard from the second-storey offices except the steady rustle of pages.

Liz read her copy three times and each time the same item caught her eye. She wasn't sure why. It wasn't the sort of target he'd chosen before. Perhaps it was only the fact that a fire there would be so comprehensive a disaster, in both financial and human terms, that set alarm bells ringing. At length she called Donovan in, hoping he could persuade her she was wrong.

'The new shopping mall?' His eyes widened as the implications sank in. 'Holy God!'

She scanned his sharp face anxiously. 'It's not me leaping to conclusions, then? You think he'll have seen that too?'

'He's bound to see it,' said Donovan, tracing the story with a long finger. 'But – I don't know, maybe it's not what he's looking for. He's never set out to hurt anyone before.'

'But he is getting more ambitious with every attack. First an empty shop; then an empty warehouse; then a thriving business after hours. A brand-new shopping mall full of people could be his next step. He's killed someone already, even if he didn't mean to. If he starts another fire after that it means he's come to terms with it: thought about it and decided it doesn't matter. If that didn't stop him he won't stop till we get him.'

Donovan was still reading. 'I can see how he'd be tempted. If he lives locally he must have seen the building going up. He must know it's about ready to open. It's a big project, they're going to town on it: celebrity cutting the ribbon, bands, fireworks, the lot. To make the most of the fireworks they've opted for a gala evening. That'll suit him fine: he likes the night, it hides him and it shows off his work. OK, with all those people about it'll be harder for him to vanish. But with all those people about, why should he? He just joins the crowd and who's to say he's not there looking round the new shops too? It'll be a nightmare to police.'

'Maybe we shouldn't try,' said Liz. 'Maybe we should get them to put it off until we find him.'

Donovan raised sceptic eyes. 'When's that likely to be?'

She found Superintendent Taylor reading the *Courier* too. She wondered if he'd spotted the same story and come to the same conclusion. But no; he was studying the photographs of the fire at the wharf. 'Shapiro,' he mused as Liz took the chair he indicated. 'Is that Frank's son?'

She nodded. 'He's a photographer – that's what he does.'

'I thought he'd moved away.'

'He lives in London. I think he was just visiting when this happened. He was staying with Donovan.'

'Sergeant Donovan?'

Liz smiled faintly. 'Don't tell me there are two.'

'That's where he lives, isn't it? Where he keeps that boat of his?'

'Right there: she was almost sunk when the wall came down.'

'So young Shapiro was perfectly placed to get his photos.' He peered at the front page. 'Too close for comfort, though.'

'He's ambitious, out to impress. Sir, while you've got the paper there turn to page three. The item on the new shopping mall.'

Taylor studied it, the neat beard bobbing as he scanned the lines. 'Yes?'

She explained what she feared. 'If he really is choosing targets from the paper, that could be irresistible. It's a major development, there's been a lot of prior publicity and they're making a big thing of the opening. Including fireworks. He won't be able to resist fireworks.'

Taylor shot her a look that was nothing less than

83

appalled. She found it rather touching that a policeman of his experience could still be shocked by the idea that people committed stupid, pointless, dangerous crimes. 'The place'll be packed with people. Shoppers, sightseers – people'll take their children!'

'Yes,' said Liz. 'If a fire starts, even quite a small one, the panic will cause more casualties than the flames. The opening's scheduled for Monday evening. That gives us the weekend to find this man and I doubt if that's possible, sir. I think we have to ask them to delay the opening; or if they won't do that, at least to hold it at a different time. At ten in the morning maybe he wouldn't be so interested.'

Superintendent Taylor had recovered his composure and doubt was creeping in. 'Do you not think you're overreacting, Liz? I mean, it's all very hypothetical. You've no actual reason to believe that the Castle Mall is his next target. Not the kind of reason I could explain to a shopping centre management who'd lose a small fortune by changing their plans now. I appreciate you're trying to second-guess this man; but an uneasy feeling hardly constitutes a threat to public safety.'

He was, Liz had recognized soon after coming to Castlemere, a man of limited imagination. But his reasoning was unassailable. She had no concrete evidence, no circumstantial evidence even, that the shopping mall was at risk. Her gut feelings had a good track record but she couldn't expect thousands of pounds to be thrown away on them alone.

'What about changing the time? Will you ask them to do that?'

He gave an elegant little shrug. 'I'll ask them. But we may have to accept that it's a bit late in the day even for that. They'll have made arrangements, booked entertainers, caterers . . . And if they ask me to make it official, I'd have trouble doing that. I'll put it to them, but I wouldn't feel justified in twisting their arms.

'Look on the bright side. By Monday night you may have it all wrapped up. If not, we'll put on a show of strength at the Castle Mall – for your peace of mind and mine – enough to make sure that everyone's there for the shops and the bands and no one's brought his own fireworks. What do you think? Will that serve?'

Liz remained uneasy. 'I can see it's maybe the best we're going to do. But, sir, I don't know how we set about effectively policing something like that, given the size of the place, and the number of people who'll be there. They won't have tickets, they won't be known to anyone. They'll all be travelling in different directions, coming and going as the mood takes them. They'll have shopping baskets, trolleys, prams and pushchairs. There'll be people on their own and family groups. There'll be gangs of teenagers and old men on sticks.

'And one of them – man, woman, adult, adolescent – will be carrying the means to start a fire. I know, I can't prove that, but it's what I believe. He'll be there. He won't be able to stay away. It's a disaster in the making. And you're telling me there's nothing we can do to prevent it?'

Taylor's smile was growing a little stiff. 'You could catch him, Inspector.'

'I am working on it,' she said reproachfully. 'In spite of the fact that we've had three fires now there isn't that much to go on. I have a line of inquiry but I'm a long way from making an arrest.'

Taylor seemed unduly impressed. 'You are making progress, then.'

Liz gave a noncommittal shrug. 'We're trying to find out where he bought the fuel he started the fires with. If we can get a description of him, then we'll have a chance.'

It was on the tip of her tongue to say that the idea was Shapiro's, that she'd talked to him about this. But she imagined that when Taylor sent someone on holiday he expected that person to get on with his gardening, decorate his house or visit relatives, not to continue as if nothing had changed except the view from his desk. Instead she said, 'When can we expect Mr Shapiro back?'

'When this other matter's cleared up,' Taylor said coolly.

'How's it going? I know we have plenty to do but I could find you some help if that would speed it up. It would be an investment really: the sooner Mr Shapiro's back, the sooner we'll get a result in the arson case.'

Taylor compressed his lips. 'We all feel the same way, Inspector. But some things take time. Thank you for your offer but I don't believe I need take you up on it. Nobody's indispensable, not even Frank Shapiro.'

'I don't think he's done a damn thing about it!' Liz exploded in the privacy of her own office – Shapiro's office – with only Donovan to hear. 'I swear to God, he has all the sense of urgency of a giant panda on its wedding night!'

'You know,' Donovan said slowly, 'I could maybe get things moving a bit.'

'You could? How?'

He made a little grimace. 'This supposed new evidence. There can't be that many people it could have come from: someone Foot knew, who's still around, who has at least some credibility else God wouldn't have done what he did. I mean, you ask a detective chief inspector to go on holiday, you need a pretty good reason.'

'So?'

'So if there's someone in town still carrying a torch for Foot after all this time, who cares enough about him to risk making a phoney allegation against the chief, I can find her.'

Alarm bells jangled. Liz raised her head and fixed him with a steely eye. 'Sergeant, I hope you're not offering to intimidate a witness.'

She'd misunderstood. Donovan looked indignant. 'Away on. Only, you and I both know there's no truth in

86

this. If we knew who was behind it we could probably nail it there and then. If she's Foot's friend – if it is a woman – she's probably about as reliable. Maybe she's done something like this before. When he knows the sort of witness he's dealing with even God'll see this is accountability gone mad, and we'll have the chief back by close of play.'

Liz was tempted. She thought he was probably right and the name of this surprise witness would tell Shapiro everything he needed to know. But she had offered CID's help and Taylor had rejected it: to send Donovan to investigate now would be as near insubordination as made no difference.

She shook her head. 'It's in Mr Taylor's hands, I think we have to let him get on with it. Maybe I'm wrong: maybe he is making progress, he just doesn't want to talk about it. Anyway, I can't spare you. We've got to make some kind of breakthrough with these fires, and we've got to do it before Monday night.'

Donovan gave his wolfish grin. 'Boss, I'm touched. You don't think you can manage without me?'

She scowled. 'I'm a detective inspector, I'm entitled to have someone to shout at. It's in my contract.'

'So shout at Scobie. It'd do him good.'

'Constables don't count – everybody shouts at them. The canteen lady shouts at Scobie.'

'That's 'cause he pinches her bread rolls for his Dolly Parton impression.'

Scobie was as tall as Donovan and twice as far round, and his nose had been broken twice before he left school. Liz didn't even want to think about his party piece. 'Get out of here. Come back when you can tell me where our arsonist bought his petrol.'

Her next visitor arrived so soon after Donovan had left that they must have passed in the corridor; a coincidence that would have been more interesting had either known who the other was. Asil Younis was looking for blood, and the blood he wanted was Donovan's.

His complexion was dark with anger: a European would have been red in the face. But he kept his anger bridled, didn't let his voice rise and sat when Liz asked him to. His self-command was impressive.

'I wish to make a serious complaint, Inspector Graham,' he began. 'It is one thing to question me, and indeed Mr Aziz, about the fires which occurred at our respective properties. I may not like the suggestion that I might know something about these incidents, but I can see that it is a legitimate line of inquiry you must pursue. I have no objection to this.

'What I do object to, most strenuously, is your sergeant bringing up a personal matter concerning my son and Mr Aziz's daughter. These two young people both have their futures to consider, and for a Pakistani – either a young man or a girl – a future without honour is barren. Your sergeant's behaviour is an insult to my family and that of Mr Aziz.'

For a moment Liz quickened at the idea that the two men were, whatever their differences, still close enough for Aziz to warn Younis about Donovan's visit. But the news had travelled a more devious route. Aziz had told his daughter that the police had been asking about her unwise friendship, Nazreen had phoned Reading to tell Fakhar Younis and Fakhar had called his father.

Liz moved smoothly into mollifying mode. 'I'm sorry if you feel our enquiries have infringed on delicate personal territory. It's not our intention to embarrass anyone over matters unconnected with the case. But I hope you can see that establishing the precise relationship between your two families, which neither you nor Mr Aziz was prepared to spell out, was important. Now we know what the situation is I see no need for it to be mentioned again. Sergeant Donovan never discussed it with anyone except Mr Aziz and me. I'm sorry if you were upset but there's no reason for you to feel insulted.'

Younis wasn't quite ready to leave it at that. 'I accept what you say, Inspector Graham. It might have been wiser if I had been candid with you in the first instance. However, there must be no more discussion of my son's friendship for Nazreen Aziz. If I hear gossip about them from any other source I shall assume that it originated here and make a formal complaint. I shall also take it as a personal affront if Sergeant Donovan comes near either myself or Mr Aziz again.'

Liz sighed. 'Mr Younis, you must know I can't let people pick and choose who they're interviewed by.'

Younis stood up, a small man with an air of infinite authority. 'I believe I have made myself clear, Inspector Graham. I shall not be in touch again. If I have further cause for complaint my solicitor will inform your superintendent.'

In which case, Liz thought glumly as she watched him go, there'll be me, DC Scobie and the canteen lady left to find a mad bastard with a box of matches before he sets fire to a shopping mall with a thousand people inside.

2

The diver found an oil can on the mud floor of the canal within a couple of minutes of going in off Broad Wharf. He started searching – groping rather than looking, the water was the colour and consistency of Brown Windsor soup – at the edge of the scree where the timberyard wall avalanched in. If the arsonist had dumped his container directly behind the building it was now lost under a hundred tons of masonry, so the diver began his search where a can might possibly have survived and very soon he found one.

Soon afterwards he found another. While he was wondering which of these two was the genuine article he found a third and fourth, and a fifth tripped him up as he made for the bank.

'Doesn't anybody round here use dustbins?' demanded Liz indignantly.

The diver pulled the breathing tube out of his mouth. 'Do you want me to keep searching, ma'am?' It was still barely mid-morning.

'Let's have a good sniff first.'

Four of the five smelled of mud, of weed, of things that had died and things that had fed on them. But one still smelled faintly of petrol. It was the can most likely in other ways too. It was a good size and shape to carry: if a man had walked into a garage and said he'd run out of petrol, the attendant would have pumped a gallon into just such an oil can for him to take back to his car. Like

90

the others it had been scratched and dented but its scars were fresher. One of the five couldn't have been used for years, corrosion having eaten away at it like leprosy. The screw-cap of another was rusted solid.

'Where did you find this one?'

The diver pointed. 'About a metre out.' A man leaving the timberyard by the side door and heading up the towpath towards the town centre would have passed the spot.

'Wrap it up for now,' decided Liz. 'I'll get this over to forensics, see how recently it's been used.'

Forensics couldn't say if it was the can used to start the fire. They could say it had been in the water for a few days; prior to that it had held petrol; and under the mud it was suspiciously clean, as if someone had wiped it down before throwing it away. The fear of leaving fingerprints seemed the only explanation for such obsessive tidiness.

Encouraged, Liz sent DCs Scobie and Morgan, armed with photographs of the can, to trawl the local filling stations. They didn't come back with a description of the arsonist, his name and the number of his credit card, but they discovered something significant. None of the mechanics had seen that precise design of can before. When Morgan contacted the distributors he was told it was a new promotion, had only been on sale for three weeks and must have been bought in the Manchester area since it wouldn't be on sale nationwide for another week.

Liz pondered that. 'So we're looking for someone with business or personal connections in or north of Manchester, who's been there in the last three weeks, who presumably has a car because I can't see him bringing a can of oil home on the train. He may be the arsonist, or he may just be a chap who bought and used some oil, then dumped the can where the arsonist could find it. Do we know anything else about him?'

'If he's a commercial traveller,' said Donovan, 'we know three nights in the last week when he was at home. I'll call the Chamber of Commerce, get a list of local firms with reps travelling to the north, then see if any of them has been in Manchester in the last month but not this week.'

'Yes, good,' agreed Liz. 'If he is a rep we should find him that way.'

'What if he's a grocer with an aunty in Oldham?'

She glowered at him. 'In that case, Sergeant, you'll need another bright idea, preferably before Monday.'

Shapiro walked to the shop for his paper. Usually he drove but this morning he needed time to think.

Last night he'd been furious. He'd felt betrayed, by his own son, and somehow that hurt more than if it had been one of his colleagues. If it had been Donovan he'd have bawled him out and then accepted that, however crazy the action, he meant well. If it had been Liz he'd have asked her reasons and considered the possibility that her judgement was better than his.

When he realized that the story in the *Courier* must have come from David, that he'd put it on the table alongside his prints as part of the deal – which was why Gail Fisher had been surprised Shapiro didn't know about it – all his tolerance deserted him. The man whose ability to remain reasonable under provocation was legendary blew his top at his son for doing something he'd already decided was less than a disaster.

Even as he was doing it he knew it was a bad move. In the last couple of days they'd made a tentative start towards repairing the damage they'd inflicted on each other. What David had done had been thoughtless at best, but Shapiro had escalated the conflict from a minor skirmish to the brink of war.

As so often in the past, David fought him not with words but with silence. His face grew white and his nostrils pinched in the face of his father's anger but he made no attempt to defend himself. Even lying would have been something: they could have argued then. But he just clenched his jaw against the onslaught and took it, and though his eyes grew hot and his breathing ragged he declined to trade in the same currency of insults and accusations, or even to answer them.

When finally in desperation Shapiro demanded, 'Have you *nothing* to say?' he only said through his teeth, 'No.' Shapiro left him alone then, defeated once again by his son's wilful refusal to communicate.

He lay awake fretting half the night, and was a little surprised to see David's van still in the drive when he woke on Friday morning. Whether it would still be there when he got back from the shop remained to be seen.

He thought he owed David an apology, not for what he'd said so much as how he'd said it. He was sure David owed him an apology, but thought he was as likely to get one from Crusher Beasley, postmarked the Isle of Wight, for bending the bars of his holding cell with the custody officer's head.

In a way, what they said was less important than the fact that they needed to talk, calmly and without recrimination. Shapiro wanted to know why David had done it, and wanted David to know why he felt hurt. But he knew now, walking back with his paper and a loaf of bread under his arm, that even that simple task was beyond them. Either they'd row – or he'd row while David went silently white – or they'd make no further reference to it, in which case David might stay another day or two but conversation would be limited to guarded exchanges over the marmalade. When he left he would disappear back into the vacuum from which mere chance had drawn him, the unexpected opportunity they had almost taken advantage of squandered.

It wasn't what he wanted. He didn't think it was what David wanted either or he wouldn't be here, he'd have stayed on Donovan's boat despite the discomfort. But the master of the subtle perceptive interview didn't know how to get from where they were to where they wanted to be.

The first thing he saw as he turned the corner of his street was that the van was still outside his house; and the second thing he saw was that the back doors were open and David was packing his gear inside. Shapiro's heart quickened and then fell in the space of about three seconds. 'You're leaving, then?'

'My job's on again. He called while you were out: he's back from the Cumbrian badgers and wants me there as soon as possible.'

'Will you be back tonight?'

David didn't glance up. He continued loading his belongings steadily into the van. 'No, he's putting me up. That was the original plan, so that I could follow him round for a few days while he did all the fascinating things that make up the life of a famous naturalist. Bird-spotting from his kitchen window, all that stuff. Crap, really, but it'll make cosy little pictures to show that even celebrities are human, they have to fit their work round the washing-up.'

'And when you're finished there?'

'Then I can go home and do something important.'

'Home to London?'

Finally David looked round at him. 'Dad, what is it you want from me? Last night you accused me of wrecking your career, this morning you want us to be friends and write and visit and all that family stuff; and I don't know why. Why can't you just accept that we don't get on? That we have nothing in common: not what's important to us, not what we do about it. That for whatever reason and whoever's to blame, we never meet without rubbing one another the wrong way.

'Can't you see it doesn't matter any more? It was hard when we had to live together, but now it doesn't matter: you can hate my guts with a clear conscience. But it would be easier on both of us if you'd accept that there's nothing left between us: there never was much and now there's nothing, and a card with a few lines inside it every

94

Chanukkah and a postcard from somewhere warm each summer is about the best we're going to do. Stop pretending we're a family. There isn't a Shapiro family any more; and even when there was I wasn't part of it.'

For a moment Shapiro stood literally open mouthed. He'd never heard David speak so plainly, or so woundingly. He could have said – should have said – 'I don't hate you, David, I never did.' He should have said, 'I never meant to hurt you.' He could even have said, 'It matters as much now as ever it did: I don't want us to be strangers for the rest of my life.' But he was taken aback and let the moment pass.

And then the previous night's anger stirred again in him. He said thickly, 'I don't know why I let you get to me. You're nothing but trouble, David, I think you always were. I was glad to see you. I was glad of the chance to put it all behind us: the misunderstandings, the bitterness. And you spat in my face. Well, that's all right. I handle rubbish every day, the smell washes off. But let's have one thing straight. Nobody cut you out of our family except you. You had everything the girls had: the same affection, the same opportunities. The only difference was that they gave something back.'

But David had said all he intended to. He twitched his father a thin-lipped smile, got into his van and drove away.

When Liz told Donovan about the visit of the irate Mr Younis and his parting threat, it was mostly for the entertainment value and just a little as a warning. She saw the way his eyes went smoky and calculating, and puzzled over it and failed to comprehend what it meant. She decided, unwisely in the event, that it probably didn't matter.

3

His trawl of the Chamber of Commerce netted four travelling salesmen who were in the Manchester area at the right time. Donovan went to see them all that Friday afternoon, starting with the representative of Castle Card & Board. Not because Mrs Lynn Markham fitted the profile of a pyromaniac – an occupation pursued by more young men than stoutish fifty-year-old grandmothers, as indeed is commercial travelling – but because Castle Card & Board was a subsidiary of Cornmarket Trading and Cornmarket Trading was owned by Asil Younis. When he told Liz he was going to see some reps Donovan omitted to mention this.

It was hard to imagine Mrs Markham setting fire to buildings for the pleasure of watching the flames mount and the Fire Brigade wade in. She might have been the headmistress of a primary school or a breeder of one of the sportier types of dog. She wore her iron-grey hair in a pudding-basin bob and dressed in comfortable, rather mannish tweeds and walking brogues.

Which might have led the casual observer, accustomed to women executives in sharp-cut suits, to think Mrs Markham was filling in for a recent departure, was related to the owner or had got her position by outstaying everyone else in the firm. Until he saw the framed certificates on her wall which catalogued an outstanding sales career of more than twenty years. She'd been the Cornmarket group's Salesperson of the Year on more occasions than

Donovan had time to count; she'd regularly won awards from the Chamber of Commerce and was twice in the last three for national honours. She might look like the organizer of Castlemere Women's Institute annual Painted Knee competition but she was a highly effective professional seller who was single-handedly responsible for a significant portion of the Cornmarket Trading Company's profits each year.

Which was a problem as well as an opportunity. If Lynn Markham had been working for almost any other firm in town she'd have been bottom of Donovan's list of suspects even if she'd been a known collector of interesting oil cans. The fact that she worked for Asil Younis altered the complexion of the thing in a way he couldn't ignore.

Even so, by the time they'd talked for five minutes he was ready to accept that it was no more than random coincidence. She gave him the dates of her trips north, confirmed that she'd been through Manchester since the new can came on the market. She had also been around Castlemere for the last ten days. But when she told him she hadn't bought a can of oil, that she never bought cans of oil, that when her BMW needed oil it went into the garage and came back not merely serviced but also valeted, Donovan believed her.

Which was unfortunate, because he wanted to go on talking to her long enough to be sure that Asil Younis would hear of it. He had to pretend an interest in pressed paper products to keep her chatting until people began to notice. He didn't leave her office until she'd diverted several phone calls and was close to selling him half a ton of corrugated paper.

With four people to see, experience told him that whatever order he took them in, whether he went alphabetically or geographically or picked with a pin, the only one with anything useful to contribute would be the last. So he went from Castle Card & Board to the nearest of the other firms, Burton Warren Light Engineering, without calculating the percentages.

The MGB was parked outside the office. It was hard to miss: a classic car in pristine condition, its livery of British Racing Green glowing with generations of wax lovingly applied. As he watched a man of about forty with an aluminium briefcase climbed in. It was a stupid car for a rep – although presumably an engineering company's salesman carries specifications rather than samples – but Donovan backed his hunch and loped over to intercept the car before it drove off.

'I'm looking for the Head of Sales, Edward Burton.'

'I'm Ted Burton. How can I help you?'

They talked in the car. Burton offered to take Donovan inside, but an office is only an office while an MGB is a star.

'You were in Manchester at the end of last month.'

'That's right. I had a couple of calls to make, I stayed at the Midland, came home the next day. What's this about?'

Donovan didn't answer directly. 'Car like this must take a lot of looking after.'

Burton blinked, then nodded. 'Sure. It's not just transport, it's a hobby. I'm underneath her most weekends.'

Donovan grinned faintly. 'Sounds more like a mistress.'

Burton laughed. His round, open face was dusted with freckles. 'You've been talking to my wife.'

'You do the work on her yourself, then.'

'Most of it. I am an engineer, after all. And there's still a surprisingly good supply of parts. I wouldn't tackle anything really major, but I do all the routine maintenance.'

'Including an oil change?'

'Of course including an oil change. Sergeant, what is all this about? What are you accusing me of?' Burton was growing tetchy but seemed genuinely puzzled: he really didn't seem to comprehend.

'Did you buy a can of oil when you were in Manchester?'

His eyes popped with surprise. 'How the hell did you know that? You've been watching me? Why, for God's sake?'

Donovan refused to be drawn. 'That's a long way to go for oil.'

'The garage proprietor's an MGB owner too. We meet at rallies, I know him – I always drop in if I'm passing. He's the expert, after all: if I buy for mine what he uses in his I'm not going to go far wrong, am I?'

'Have you used it yet?'

Burton gave up trying to understand, just answered. 'As a matter of fact I have. Last weekend. Sunday morning, to be precise.'

'What did you do with the empty can?'

'I threw it away!'

'Where?'

Burton rolled his eyes. 'You expect me to remember that?' Then his voice altered. 'As a matter of fact, I do remember. I put it in the skip. They've been laying pipes in the service lane behind my house, there's been a skip there for weeks. My bin was full so I dumped the can in the skip. All right?'

'Where do you live, Mr Burton?'

'Cambridge Road.'

Probably it meant nothing. Cambridge Road ran for miles into the countryside. But still Donovan felt the need to ask. 'You're not by any chance a neighbour of Mr Asil Younis?'

'That's right,' said Burton, finally growing angry. 'He lives two doors up on one side. And your superintendent lives three doors down on the other.'

Liz thought Taylor must have some news when he called her to his office. So he had, but it wasn't what she was hoping for. 'Did you send Sergeant Donovan to talk to Asil Younis again? After the man came here and complained about him?'

Taken aback, Liz shook her head. 'No, sir.'

'But he's been. To Mr Younis's house.'

'Really?'

'You're not aware of this?'

'I haven't seen Donovan since this morning. He went looking for the owner of the oil can we found in the canal, the one that had held petrol.'

'Why would he think it belonged to Mr Younis?'

'I don't know,' admitted Liz. 'But he must have had something in mind.' Under Taylor's sceptical gaze she amended that. 'Well, he may have had something in mind. I'll find out.'

There was a long silence. But Taylor didn't seem to be thinking about it; Liz thought he'd reached a decision before calling her in. 'I'd like you to reassign him.'

Her eyes flew wide in surprise. 'Take him off the case?'

'There must be other things he can do, other cases requiring attention. It seems to me he's lost his objectivity over this one and you'll make more progress without him getting people's backs up.'

Liz couldn't believe they were having this conversation. She wasn't that surprised Donovan had found or manufactured a reason to see Younis again. She wasn't surprised Younis had complained about it: he'd said he would, she took him for a man of his threats. And of course he and Taylor would be known to one another, being near neighbours on one of the very best stretches of Cambridge Road. She might have expected a gentle tweaking of strings.

But she didn't expect to be told to drop her sergeant. Superintendent Taylor knew she was anxious about how this case might develop, and the only comfort he'd been able to offer was the hope that she'd have it cleared up before Castle Mall opened. Now he expected her to pare her team down further because a local businessman, whose own integrity was by no means certain, was offended. It was absurd. She was damned if she was going to accept it.

'Sir, I don't think you can have thought this through. I'm already struggling without DCI Shapiro. If I sideline Donovan as well it'll be me and a bunch of constables to deal with a maniac who's effectively holding this town to ransom.'

Taylor's manner was cool. 'You're exaggerating, Inspector.'

'Forgive me, sir, but I'm not. If he's still at large by Monday night he's going to be at the shopping precinct. So are thousands of other people. You say we can't get the opening deferred, and we both know that the chances of normal policing picking him out of the crowd are tiny. Now you're telling me that because he's upset a suspect – all right, a long shot of a suspect but somebody who's certainly involved – I should send Donovan to check shotgun licences and the serial numbers on videos. I can't afford to, sir. I need his help.'

Taylor let a well-shaped eyebrow arch in mannerly disbelief. 'You're telling me you can't run your department without Detective Sergeant Donovan holding your hand?'

Liz bristled. 'Of course I'm not. I'm saying that, whatever his social failings, he's an experienced detective with a good track record and I need more like him not less. I'll find out why he went to see Younis again. If necessary I'll drag him over the coals. With your permission, sir, I'll tell him of this conversation so he's in no doubt about how seriously we're taking Younis's complaints. But I can't afford to weaken my grip on this.' She took a deep breath and went on the record. 'I'm sorry, sir, but if you want him off the case it'll have to be an order. If the discretion is mine I won't part with him.'

Superintendent Taylor sighed. 'Liz, I don't want to pull rank on you. You're doing a good job in difficult circumstances and I want to help. I don't want to undermine your authority.'

She'd come this far, she might as well say what was on her mind. 'Forgive me, sir. But I don't think you'd be having this conversation with Mr Shapiro. I think you'd accept his judgement as to how and when to discipline his officers, and when an investigation is important enough to risk a little flak. If you're satisfied with the job I'm doing, won't you trust me to get on with it?'

Again the long pause while he formulated his reply. But it wasn't the content he was considering so much as the packaging. 'I've run Queen's Street for a good few years now. It's a more complex job than it perhaps appears. There are different interests to reconcile, of which thief-taking is only one. We need the support of the community to succeed, and that means not alienating important sections of it by being unnecessarily thoughtless, or clumsy, or rude. Mr Younis may be a member of a racial minority but—'

Liz was not an impetuous woman. Self-control had proved its worth on her climb through the ranks of her profession. So she didn't make a habit of interrupting senior officers; but this time she made an exception. 'Sir, if you think Sergeant Donovan would have behaved differently if Mr Younis had been white, without knowing any of the details I feel quite safe in saying that you're wrong. Donovan is many things, not all of them admirable. But he's not a bigot.'

'I'm very glad to hear it,' said Taylor. 'It shouldn't, of course, need saying but we're both aware that it has become an issue in the job today. Well, you work with him closer than I do, I'll accept your assessment. The fact remains, Mr Younis believes he was the victim of discrimination.'

'By taking Donovan off the inquiry you're as good as confirming it.'

'No, I'm avoiding an unnecessary confrontation. That's what I mean about reconciling different interests. Perceived failings can do as much damage as real ones. If nothing else, Donovan needs to learn discretion. And we have to be seen to be alive to the sensibilities of those we serve. I'm sorry if you feel it'll be a problem, but in all the circumstances I don't consider it appropriate for Sergeant Donovan to continue on this inquiry. If you don't wish to convey that message to him I'll tell him myself.'

Little as she liked it, Liz had no choice but to accept his decision. 'No, I'll tell him, sir. But I would like to put on record my view that the action is unjustified.'

Taylor nodded, the least trace of a smile in the curve of his beard. 'So noted, Inspector. Now, if you'll excuse me, I have a lot of work . . .'

So had Liz; more than before she came in here. Still she lingered. 'The Foot business?'

'That too,' said Taylor flatly; and he held her eyes and said nothing more until finally, defeated, she excused herself and left.

4

Donovan heard her out in silence, itself a suspicious sign. By the time she'd finished there was the ghost of a smile on his thin lips. She shut her eyes a moment to collect her thoughts. 'Would you care to tell me what's going on?'

His face wasn't designed to do ingenuous but that didn't stop him trying occasionally. 'Nothing's going on. I found out where the oil can came from, I was told it was dumped in a skip a hundred metres from Younis's house and Younis stands to gain from one of the fires. I had every reason to see him again.'

'Why didn't you tell me first?'

He shrugged in what he believed to be a nonchalant manner. 'I was in the area, I thought I'd call on my way back.'

It all sounded quite sensible but Liz knew none of this had just happened, he'd planned it for reasons she hadn't yet fathomed. 'You knew how he felt about you. You must have known how he'd react to you turning up at his door.'

'Mm,' admitted Donovan.

'Now he's complained to God and God wants you off the case. I tried to argue but he pulled rank on me. So I came up here to break the news gently, and now I see this is what you wanted all along. Why?'

'You said yourself, we need the Chief back.'

Liz stared. 'How's it going to get the Chief back to have you watching from the sidelines?'

'If I have some time, maybe I can get to the bottom of the Foot business. For all I can see, nobody else is trying to.'

After working with him for twelve months she could still be startled by his effrontery. 'Absolutely not! I have a direct instruction from Superintendent Taylor to keep out of that. If it applies to me, it sure as hell applies to you.'

'Yes, OK,' he said casually.

Liz wasn't fooled. He didn't agree that easily to anything he actually intended doing. She scowled. 'I can't believe you did that. You know the trouble we're in: how little time we've got, how far we are from a result. How much I need all hands on deck. I can't believe you've been so irresponsible.'

His face grew stubborn, his accent as always thickening under pressure. 'I didn't plan it. Not exactly. It just occurred to me that, if this was the outcome, it wouldn't be altogether disastrous. The sooner the Chief's back, the sooner we'll nail this madman.'

Sometimes she almost despaired of him. There was in his make-up as a policeman, perhaps in the orientation of his brain, a slight deviation like the difference between grid and magnetic north. It wasn't huge: for much of the time his mind, like a compass needle, was true enough for all practical purposes. But on occasions this gap appeared – like a narrow, very deep chasm – as between police procedure and how Donovan did things. It was impossible to get him in line by explaining things. It was a waste of energy arguing with him, though she did it often enough. A direct unambiguous order stood a chance of curbing him, though not if he felt strongly enough.

He got away with it – in so far as he did, it was already there in his record and meant he wouldn't see another promotion – because (a) he genuinely cared about getting the job done regardless of the cost to himself; and (b) when he was right he could achieve things no one else could.

Liz said, 'What about Younis and the oil can?'

'He said he hadn't touched it, of course. He said if he wanted an oil can he'd got plenty of his own without rooting through other people's skips.'

'Did you believe him?'

Donovan shrugged. 'I don't know. It's a hell of a coincidence that we can trace the can used to set one fire almost to the back garden of another victim of the same arsonist. But Younis has no motive we know of to burn the timberyard; and even if he had I can't see him wandering his back lane on the off-chance of finding the means. I guess I do believe him.'

'Where does that leave us?'

Donovan sketched a line at about eye-level with the side of his hand. 'About up to here in the—?'

'Thank you, Sergeant,' Liz said quickly. 'Go and do something useful. Pick up on some of the stuff we left off when all this started. Stay away from Asil Younis. Stay away from God.' She dropped her eyes to the papers in front of her. 'And if you can't stay away from the Foot business you'd better be damn sure you're on your own time.'

Donovan could have pulled the file on Trevor Foot but not without word reaching Superintendent Taylor. Despite often behaving in ways that made people wonder, he wanted to keep his job. And he didn't want Liz taking his flak. He knew she gave him more leeway than was customary – had wondered, in his sourer moments, if it were not so much leeway as rope – and didn't want to repay that by dragging her down with him when he finally pushed his luck too far.

So the files were out of bounds. The Foot case was closed before he came to Castlemere so he couldn't raid his own memory; and asking someone who'd been here longer would have the same effect as consulting the file – it would get back to God. So he went straight to the horse's mouth.

Shapiro was surprised to see him. It was a little after 8 p.m. and, knowing how CID was fixed, he'd thought they'd be burning midnight oil. 'Time off for good behaviour?'

Donovan looked shifty. 'Not exactly.'

Shapiro had known him long enough to be able to tell when Donovan was up to something a respectable police officer wouldn't want to know about. It would be politic, he thought, to stay well away from whatever it was that was making him glance about as if someone might be following him. After all, Shapiro was on holiday, specifically debarred from engaging in police business for a week or so.

With a sigh he opened the door wide. 'Come in. Tell me about it.'

He reacted as Liz had done: with disbelief, anger, finally with resignation. 'You don't need me to tell you this is not a good career move.'

Donovan's lip curled. 'Careers are for inspectors and above. Sergeants have jobs. My current job is looking for three televisions, two VCRs and a dish-washer that walked after a van hit the window of Pearson's Electrical while trying to avoid a Staffordshire bull terrier. I'll do it, but I won't work sixteen hours a day to do it. This is my off-time.'

'If you succeed in discrediting this witness, Mr Taylor's going to have to know. Have you thought what you'll say then?'

Donovan didn't see a problem. 'I'll tell him the truth. Once he knows it's only one loony out to avenge another, that'll be the end of your holiday.'

Shapiro had never been a slave to procedure but he paled at the risk Donovan was running. If it didn't work out there'd be hell to pay. If it did work out Taylor would hold it against him for as long as they were both in Castlemere. 'Maybe. But he won't like you for it.'

The younger man sniffed. 'He doesn't like me now.'

Against his better judgement Shapiro began to smile.

107

'It's not that he doesn't like you, Donovan. It's more that you offend him. Your hair's too long. You lean on things. You spit in the eye of convention. In spite of all this you're a good copper. He finds that most offensive of all.'

There was no doubt in Shapiro's mind what he should do: thank Donovan for his offer, send him back to his missing electricals with the advice that he should do what he was told and let those paid to decide the comparative importance of inquiries get on with it.

The snag was, that wasn't what he wanted to do. Like Donovan he thought Taylor was making some poor decisions. He didn't see why he had to leave Queen's Street at the height of a crisis. Perhaps the allegation against him did need investigating, but he couldn't think what was taking so long. He'd heard nothing for two days. He hadn't been asked any questions yet. What kind of inquiry was it that didn't involve interviewing the suspect?

So he warmed to the idea of someone on his side looking at the matter. He knew Donovan couldn't close the case, but he could speed the process that would put Castlemere's DCI back where he belonged. Feeling that way coaxed him into a dubious decision of his own. He persuaded himself that what Donovan was doing wasn't really insubordination, and that the end would in any event justify the means.

'All right. But for pity's sake be discreet. All I need to know is who's produced this photograph and what it's supposed to show. It has to be someone close to Foot: the chances are that if I had the name I could tell Taylor just how much his new evidence is worth.'

'I'll get you a name,' promised Donovan. 'But I need somewhere to start – I know nothing about the case. Tell me what happened.'

It was the mid-Eighties, there was a lot of Awareness about. Fur coats were out, ozone was in and people marched in Whitehall with inflatable whales. Some people felt so strongly about man's inhumanity to animals that they were prepared to commit mayhem on people who felt differently.

BioMedical Technology was a commercial research laboratory which, because it held a Home Office licence for animal experiments, attracted a campaign of protests which became increasingly violent over a span of about three months. It began with graffiti on the walls and progressed to paint on the director's car and threats in the post. Matters reached a head when the director, exasperated and genuinely believing in the necessity of his work, decided he'd kept a low profile long enough and went on television to put his case.

Anticipating trouble, Castlemere's newly arrived DCI Shapiro had a squad car make regular visits to the laboratory. The following evening at dusk a van drew up outside and men in balaclavas got out. Then, finding themselves under police surveillance, they piled back in the van and took off at speed.

After three miles of hot pursuit, suddenly the van pulled over. The driver claimed he hadn't realized the car behind was a police vehicle, had thought it was just anxious to overtake. The men in balaclavas were a student darts team with the arrows and a small silver trophy to prove it. They had a fixture against a local pub but the driver had lost his way.

Though it was plainly a decoy, Shapiro could never prove the connection between those in the van and what happened at BMT. The planning was meticulous. The match was genuine, the other team waiting in the pub. The young men in balaclavas were real darts players: they won the rearranged fixture and retained the silver cup.

But while the police were chasing the van another group was breaking into the laboratory, removing the animals and setting incendiaries. While the darts players were protesting their innocence an explosion lit up The Levels for miles around. By the time the Fire Brigade arrived BMT was reduced to cinders and an asthmatic nightwatchman was heaving his lungs out on the grass.

Because the action was claimed by BEAST in the cause of saving animals from torture there was a reluctance to condemn it even among people whose natural inclination was to support the law. When security man Stan Belshaw died two weeks later from the effects of smoke inhalation there was a feeling that it was more a misfortune than a crime.

So Shapiro was denied the co-operation he'd have had if Belshaw had been hit over the head by safe-crackers. The darts team stuck to their story of an innocent misunderstanding and Shapiro failed to identify a single member of BEAST. He believed that, like the darts team, it was primarily a student group based at Cambridge, but his enquiries were stone-walled at every turn. Everyone questioned had heard of BEAST, many approved of its aims, but no one admitted being members or knowing people who were.

Until twelve days after the raid, with Stan Belshaw still drawing ragged breath in the Intensive Care Unit at Castlemere General, when Trevor Foot was heard boasting of his involvement in the bar of the Ginger Pig.

If he was to be believed he'd had the idea, drawn up the plan, led the raid and also knitted the darts team's balaclavas. There was a general concensus that BEAST was the child of a half-mythical Herne-like figure called Red Kenny. Without exactly signing autographs, Foot left his audience in little doubt as to who Red Kenny really was. Since at that time the only acknowledged casualties of the incident were the property and profits of a company involved in vivisection, he had a not unsympathetic hearing as he described how he had outwitted the law, risking his own liberty for that of the laboratory animals.

Despite his boasts, Shapiro never believed that Foot masterminded the raid. He wasn't the type: then aged thirty, he was a small ferrety individual with a record for

110

petty theft and disturbing the peace. But he did believe he was involved. Foot had a fondness for this kind of activity – every lunatic fringe group in Castlemere had enjoyed his support at some time. The pattern never varied. He went to a meeting, got swept away with revolutionary zeal, joined, volunteered for active service, got in the way, criticized the founder members for lack of commitment and got thrown out. Before BEAST it was the National Front. Before that it was the Moonies. Shapiro reckoned that under questioning he would reveal the names of his fellow conspirators.

Foot submitted to arrest cheerfully enough. He had confessed to glamorous crimes before, been interviewed by the police and released without charge. He expected the outcome to be the same this time.

But during questioning the news came through that Stan Belshaw had died. Immediately Foot changed his story. Now he denied everything. He wasn't a member of BEAST, he didn't plan the raid, he wasn't at BMT, and he had never had too much to drink in the Ginger Pig and claimed he was.

But there were witnesses to what he'd said, and he had no alibi for the time of the raid. In fact, he'd been missing from his job as a painter and decorator all that day and the previous one. He claimed to have gone to London for a dirty midweek. He didn't know the girl's name, except that it was Sue, or where she lived except it was a tower block. He got a train home from King's Cross but didn't keep the ticket.

It was as poor an explanation for two missing days as Shapiro had ever heard from someone accused of a serious crime. Still he tried to check it. None of Foot's colleagues had heard him mention a girl named Sue. No one in the Ginger Pig saw him pick her up. No one at the station remembered him getting off the London train at about the time the raid was taking place.

Nor was it true that he knew nothing about BEAST.

111

He knew not only their aims and objectives, as anyone who read the papers might, but was also familiar with their phraseology. Expressions like 'mankind's ruthless greed' and 'sentience in all its forms' tripped off his tongue too easily for a man who claimed to know no more than had appeared in the *Courier*.

There was also forensic evidence. One of the incendiaries failed to ignite; because it was in a filing cabinet it survived the blaze intact. Analysis revealed that one of the active ingredients was paint-stripper, of a brand used in Foot's workshop.

Even if Foot wasn't a mainstay of BEAST, Shapiro hoped that he'd name those who were rather than do time for them. But he never did. He tried obvious lies – he knew nothing about BEAST, was stringing the people in the pub along. He tried a subtler mix of lies and truth – he was a minor figure in the organization, so minor he didn't know who the others were. He tried fantasy – they contacted him by means of anonymous messages left at his work. He tried righteous indignation, he tried bribery, he tried tears.

But he never tried telling the whole truth. So he was charged with arson and manslaughter, and the jury was unimpressed by his claim that he was fitted up. He got twelve years.

Donovan said, 'He must be about due for release.'

'You get remission for good behaviour,' said Shapiro. 'Trevor's been in every kind of trouble available in prison short of knifing warders. He's even been on the roof a couple of times. He can't resist joining things, even roof-top protests. He'd have been out by now if he'd kept his head down.'

'This photograph. What's it likely to be?'

Shapiro shrugged. 'I imagine it's supposed to prove that he was in London during those missing days. But we weren't shown a picture, and Foot's brief never made any

112

reference to it. I just don't believe in photographs that surface after eight years.'

'So someone doctored it to make it look like Foot was innocent,' agreed Donovan. 'Why wait till now?' But Shapiro didn't know. 'What family does he have?'

'Eight years ago he had a father in the Rosedale Nursing Home and cousins living in Cambridge. Neither were any help to him then, I don't know why they'd lie for him now.'

'What about this woman?'

'The elusive Sue?' Shapiro shook his head. 'A figment of his imagination. If she'd been real she wouldn't have waited eight years. There's nothing she can do now that she couldn't have done when this started, and it'd have looked a damn sight more convincing then.'

Donovan was thinking. 'I don't suppose I can see Foot without God finding out. Known haunts, then. The Pig, you said. And his work: where was that?'

'Willards, behind Castle Place. I suppose you could try some of his fellow cranks. The local Moonies packed up but there's still a branch of the National Front. The secretary's called Huddleston, he dates back to when Foot was a member.'

'I'll get on to it tonight.' Donovan kept it out of his voice, but in the pits of his eyes was the knowledge of how difficult this could be: picking up threads that had been eight years in the ravelling. 'I'll be in touch when I've some news.'

Shapiro saw him out. 'Sergeant, I appreciate what you're doing but don't stick your neck out too far. Sooner or later I'll be vindicated. I don't want to get back and find you're out on your ear.'

5

Nothing much had changed at the Castle Mews yard since Foot was last there. Mr Willard senior had handed over the reins of office to his son but still came in when the order books were full. A couple of apprentices had grown into journeymen but still wore the same T-shirts and made the same jokes. Foot's mug was probably still among those ranged round the kettle. If he'd come in and quietly picked up a brush, quite possibly no one would have commented.

He was remembered with a certain affection, Donovan learned from young Mr Willard who was working late on his books in the silent workshop. This was not because he was a good worker, a good mate or even a reliable source of tips for the 2.50 at Newmarket. He was lazy, undependable, slapdash, shifty and a bore. But the case had afforded them a few weeks of vicarious celebrity, and nothing more interesting had happened in Castle Mews in the eight years since.

'Had he any close friends here? People he might have kept in touch with?'

Young Mr Willard, now in his late fifties, shook his head. 'I don't think he had any friends at all, here or anywhere else. Nobody ever came asking for him or called him on the phone.'

'He claimed BEAST used to leave messages for him here.'

Willard smiled gently. 'Sergeant, the first thing we

found out about Trevor was never to believe a word he said. He was a congenital liar. Nothing ordinary ever happened to him. He never dropped the last tin of Flamenco Red: somebody pushed him or distracted him or left something to trip him up. He never took a bend too fast and scraped the van: he had to swerve to avoid a lost puppy. If you showed any sign of believing him he'd spin it out until you knew what kind of puppy it was, what colour it was and how its eyes filled with terror when it thought its last minute had come. He'd end up believing it himself. He was a fantasist, Sergeant. Real life was a disappointment so he made up something better.'

'Did you know about all these organizations he joined?'

The painter nodded ruefully. 'Oh, yes. He'd come in every few months and try to convert everyone to the new cause. It was the same as the stories: if you didn't know better you'd swear he'd finally found his life's work. But after a few weeks he'd be complaining about how the other members were letting him down and soon after that he'd come in with a silly grin and his pockets full of somebody else's literature.'

'Did you know he'd joined BEAST?'

'Actually, no. He must have been sworn to secrecy on his mother's life, normally he talked about nothing but his latest cause. And the girlfriends, of course.'

Donovan pricked his ears. 'There were girls, then.'

'None at all,' said Willard blithely. 'But he always talked as if he had Madonna and Kylie Minogue waiting for him in the Élite Café.'

'What about Sue?'

'The one he was supposed to have spent the missing days with? No such person, Sergeant. Sue was just the last in a long line of beautiful women who couldn't keep their hands off Trevor Foot. We used to say, Trevor, if you've got so many bring them here and share them round. But we never saw him with anyone except his old dad. Bit sad, really. I suppose we might have made more effort. Not that we've that much social life, any of us, but at least we don't need imaginary friends.'

'So you can't think of anyone who liked him well enough to do him a favour?' Willard shook his head. 'Did you ever hear about a photograph that might have cleared him?'

Willard looked surprised. 'I thought it was an open-and-shut case. You're not telling me he didn't do it after all?'

'No, of course not,' Donovan said quickly. 'It's just, an allegation's been made and we have to look into it. The suggestion is there was a photograph that would have helped his defence. Maybe showing Sue, I don't know.'

'Arthur Conan Doyle,' pronounced the painter thoughtfully. 'Wasn't he the last intelligent man to believe you could photograph fairies?'

Philip Huddleston wasn't the first member of the National Front Donovan had met, but he was the first who continued to treat him with a degree of civility after his name and accent revealed his origins. Usually there was a curling of thick lips, a bristling of bald heads, and somebody sang 'If You Ever Go Across The Sea To Ireland, Stay There'. Donovan wasn't easily upset by such pantomime. If he was talking to members of the National Front it usually meant he was about to arrest one of them, which kept his mood sunny.

Huddleston wasn't like that. He was a very ordinary man in his late forties, the natural thinning of his hair unassisted by a razor, not a tattoo in sight. He wore grey flannels and a tweed jacket with leather patches on the elbows. He might have been a teacher or librarian. Actually he was an aircraft safety engineer.

He remembered Trevor Foot with less affection than young Mr Willard. 'He was an odd one.'

Donovan bit his tongue. 'Why, particularly?'

Huddleston smiled thinly. 'He came to us on the rebound from the Moonies. His primary aim was the banning of Korean clergymen.'

The same questions Donovan had put to Willard produced similar answers from Huddleston. Foot had made no close friends within the branch; no one had kept in touch with him after he left; if he had a girlfriend he'd never brought her to meetings. Like Willard, Huddleston hadn't believed the story of Foot haring off to London for two days with a girl named Sue.

Also like Willard, he remembered being surprised by the BEAST connection. 'He never showed any interest in animal rights when he was with us. Our annual debate on ritual slaughter went right over his head.'

'So you were surprised he joined an animal activist group.'

'Astonished,' Huddleston said frankly. 'And even more astonished that a group like that – engaged, unlike ourselves, in illegal activities and so dependent on the discretion of its members – saw him as a suitable co-conspirator. I wouldn't like to share secrets with Trevor Foot. Especially not the kind that could put me behind bars.'

'Even when it would put him behind bars too?'

Huddleston shrugged. 'I don't think it would make any difference. Chattering was a pathological condition with him: he'd tell you everything about himself, down almost to every thought he'd ever had, within half an hour of meeting you. He was like a smoker who can't give up even when he knows it's killing him.'

It was a good point. The question was not why Trevor Foot had anything to do with BEAST but why BEAST had anything to do with Trevor Foot. 'Did you say any of this to the investigating officers?'

'I didn't get the opportunity. Nobody interviewed me.'

'Was there a different secretary then?'

'No, I've been doing this job for ten years. And don't bother to track down the chairman and treasurer for that year: the police didn't talk to them either. We discussed it at the time: we all thought it rather shoddy. Of course, we knew why.'

Donovan was puzzled. It must have showed in his face.

'Come, Sergeant,' said Huddleston briskly, 'don't be so naïve. Detective Chief Inspector Shapiro is a Jew, isn't he? He wasn't going to admit he might have something to learn from the National Front.'

The Ginger Pig was the nearest respectable pub to Queen's Street so it was effectively Donovan's local. Actually the Fen Tiger was closer but that was a villains' pub and it suited all concerned not to get drunk in mixed company.

Eight years is a long time in the life of a pub. Licensees change; regulars change; juke boxes, fruit machines, pub quizzes and wet T-shirt competitions come and go. But a middle-aged barmaid is as close to for ever as the human mind can contemplate and Doris had been dispensing pints, good humour and motherly advice for five years to Donovan's knowledge. He felt sure she'd have been at the Pig in the mid-Eighties.

'Lor' yes, dear,' she replied with a nostalgic heave of her substantial white-nylon bosom. 'I've been here thirteen years come January. The only thing that's been here longer than me's the graffiti in the gents.' She gave a coarse, good-natured laugh.

Donovan smiled dutifully. They were old acquaintances. She served him alcohol-free lager and let the other customers think he was a hard drinker. 'Do you remember Trevor Foot that used to drink in here? Before he got sent down for fire-bombing a laboratory.'

'Ooh yes, dear, I remember him. Big cider man.' Doris never forgot a drink.

'Do you remember who he drank with?'

She gave it a moment's thought, pursing her carmine lips. 'Lots of people, but only once each.'

'I was told he was a bit of a bore.'

'Listen, ducky, he could bore for England. He could beat a white-faced French mime artist into second place in the European championships of Le Boring held every

118

five years in Ostend.' For an uneducated woman Doris had a colourful turn of phrase. 'I've seen him empty this pub ten minutes into the Happy Hour. Takes some doing, that does.'

'Going on about his organizations, was he?'

'And on,' nodded Doris. 'And on, and on.'

'Was there nobody he drank with regularly? You know, a friend?'

She shrugged broad shoulders. 'Not as I recall. Some of the lads used to take the piss out of him sometimes. Pardon my French. You know, get him going and wet themselves listening to him. But I don't think even Trevor thought they were friends.'

'Were you here the night he claimed to have done the raid?' She nodded again. 'He must have thought he was among friends then.'

'I think he was just pissed, dear,' confided Doris. 'The way he was talking, it wasn't any kind of secret. Everyone in the bar must have heard.'

And someone had called the police. 'Who reported him, Doris? Was it you?'

She looked mildly embarrassed. 'No, dear, it wasn't. I would have if I'd believed him, but I thought he was spinning a line. There was a bunch of them sitting with him, egging him on – you know, "Tell us about the Moonies, Trevor, tell us about the National Front." And the attention sort of went to his head. That's what I thought, anyway. I thought he'd claim to have shot President Kennedy before they were done.'

Donovan felt the faint beginning twinges of unease. He'd set out to trace Foot's friends, friends so good they were still lying for him after eight years, and instead he kept meeting people who'd found it hard to believe that Foot had done what he was supposed to have done. 'What are you saying, Doris? That he's in jail for something he didn't do?'

'Oh no, dear,' she said, instantly and certainly. 'It was

119

Mr Shapiro's case, wasn't it? If Mr Shapiro thought he did it, and if the jury that heard all that evidence thought he did it, that's good enough for me. I mean, I'm no detective, am I? I'm a barmaid. I suppose I only ever saw him as a pathetic little man drinking cider in the corner of the lounge, so lonely he was glad of people making fun of him.'

Donovan nodded. That was probably it. The same applied to the other people he'd talked to. 'And I don't suppose you can think of anyone who'd still consider himself – or herself, a woman would do fine – as Foot's friend?'

Doris thought about it but then shook her head sadly. 'I think I may have been the closest thing Trevor had to a friend, and I haven't thought about him for years. I suppose he'll be getting out sometime soon, will he?'

Donovan was noncommittal. 'Maybe not. He seems to have joined the prison Mafia this time.'

But that wasn't quite the end of the trail. As he went to leave Doris called after him, 'You know, there was someone who'd have the odd drink with Trevor – without making fun of him, I mean. I wouldn't have called them friends but he didn't avoid Trevor the way most people did. I think they used to see one another at meetings.'

'Another crank?'

'Oh no, he's paid to do things like that. Tom Shelley, the photographer at the *Courier*.'

'Photographer?' All Donovan's alarm systems went off at once.

6

About the time Donovan was going home, having failed to think up a plausible excuse to call at a newspaper photographer's home at eleven thirty at night, David Shapiro was tracking his badger expert through Hunter's Spinney, weighed down by cameras, lenses, flashlights and the certainty that the shot Payne wanted was unobtainable. Unless they stuffed the badgers first, the chances of them staying put long enough for Keaton Payne to creep into the same shot were minimal. The film when developed contained one in-focus shot of a badger's mask and a man's hand, one of a badger's disappearing scut and Payne looking cross and nothing else that showed both man and beast.

When even the naturalist was resigned to the failure of the expedition, they repaired to Payne's house on the edge of the wood to restore their sense of humour with hot whisky.

'You're a local man, then,' said Payne when David mentioned visiting the spinney as a child. 'Any relation to our CID chief?'

David was slow to answer. 'He's my father.'

'At least you had somewhere to stay when I had to disappear.' He was a big leonine man in his thirties, tall and broad and well made without being heavy, like one of the faster brands of rugby player. He also moved like an athlete, as if he were aware of every muscle in his body. Even when he sprawled in his chair beside the fire

121

it was with a kind of fierce feline grace. 'I'm sorry about that. System must have gone all to pot. Can't blame my secretary,' he added with a disarming grin, 'I haven't got one.'

'Don't worry about it,' said David, 'the time wasn't wasted. That fire at the wharf? I was right there when it started. I got some shots you wouldn't believe.'

'For the nationals?'

'For everybody. The nationals took some, the *Courier* took some, but the best ones are going in my portfolio.' He wasn't a man to discuss his hopes with near strangers, but the whisky must have got to him because he went on talking, with increasing enthusiasm, until he heard himself and broke off, colouring, in mid-sentence.

Payne smiled at him, amused. 'Never be ashamed of your dreams. You want something, you go for it. There are too many people in this world who haven't the guts to try for something because it's difficult or risky, and it's easier to accept the status quo than to try and change things. But you can take on the world if you care enough.' He poured more whisky. 'I imagine your father found the pictures helpful too.'

Even a man who didn't make his living observing the body-language of wild creatures would have noticed that twice now David had gone still at the mention of his father. Payne elucidated. 'With the investigation. I presume he's handling it?'

'Actually no,' said David, 'he's on leave.'

Payne was surprised. 'Aren't they treating it as arson? I thought all leave was cancelled at times like this.'

'I wouldn't know,' David said coldly. 'I've never been a student of police procedure.'

Payne put the leonine head a little on one side, trying to weigh him up. 'He's well thought of in this town, your father.'

'He should be.' David put his glass down and stood up. 'I'm going to call it a night. Do you want to make an early start tomorrow?'

Payne accepted the rebuff good-naturedly. 'No need. Six o'clock'll do fine.'

On Saturday morning Donovan went to the office via Tom Shelley's house, startling his wife by handing her the milk bottles when she opened the door to take them in.

When he took off his motorcycle helmet and introduced himself, the momentary fear turned to a faint puzzled anxiety. 'What do you want with Tom?'

'A word about someone he used to know, that's all.' Partly it was his job, but it was more than that. Nobody ever looked at Donovan and thought it was good news.

By then Shelley had joined them, pulling a fawn sweater over his shirt. He was in his forties now, beginning to spread out a little, a family man with a wife, two children, a dog and a hatchback. Once he'd shared David Shapiro's dream of front-line photography, had gone on thinking he'd do it when the time was right. But quite recently it struck him that he no longer wanted to work that hard. He'd grown comfortable in the life he had.

He and Donovan knew one another casually. They'd worked on the same jobs, leaned on the same bars; he was surprised to find Donovan on his doorstep at eight in the morning but happy enough to answer his questions.

He remembered Trevor Foot. As Doris supposed, it wasn't so much a friendship as a contented man being kind to a lonely one. But Shelley had probably talked to Foot as much as anyone in Castlemere, and he was in the Ginger Pig the night Foot provided the floor-show with his famous confession. 'If you want to call it that,' said Shelley.

'What do you mean?'

The photographer shrugged. 'It's only a confession if it's true. I was never convinced Trevor Foot did what he said he did.'

'Why not?'

'For one thing, he was a lying little git.' Shelley sniffed. 'But more than that, I just didn't believe it. He was a talker, not a doer. Maybe he could have talked himself in deeper than he meant to, ended up tailing along on a raid with those people. But never if he lived to be a hundred could he have organized it.'

Donovan nodded. 'The Chief never reckoned that part of it either. The case didn't hang on him organizing it. It just needed him to be there, and the jury believed that he was.'

'Well, they'd hear more about it than I did,' said Shelley. 'But I was surprised. I know it didn't prove anything but I thought the photograph might have made them wonder.'

If someone had slapped Donovan across the head with a wet mackerel he could hardly have been more startled. For a moment he had trouble forming the words. '*What* photograph?'

'The one of Foot and his girlfriend,' said Shelley, clearly unaware that he was shaking Donovan's world. 'The one I gave Mr Shapiro.'

Liz had been up early to feed her horse and was having breakfast in the kitchen with her husband when she heard the motorbike gun to a halt in the drive. Her heart sank. Donovan was the only biker she knew who did Grand Prix stops.

Brian picked up his toast, his coffee and his newspaper and padded off to the study. 'I'll leave you to it.'

Liz looked at him in surprise. 'There's no need. It won't be anything – delicate.'

She'd misunderstood. Long-sufferingly, Brian explained. 'Every time Donovan comes here you two end up talking about dead bodies. In detail. While I'm trying to eat. What's delicate is my stomach.'

When she opened the door she thought there must have been another fire. A bad one. Most people go white with shock but Donovan went sallow and his eyes sank into his skull. That was how he looked now: like a death's head. His voice was thick with accent and emotions she couldn't identify. 'We have to talk.'

She could hardly take her eyes off his face. 'All right. Come through to the kitchen.'

There was still coffee in the pot. Automatically she put a mug in front of him, as if he'd been in an accident. 'What's happened?'

He folded long hands round the warm mug but made no attempt to drink. 'We – miscalculated. There was a girl. There was a photograph of Foot with the girl, and the Chief had it.'

Then she understood his expression. She too felt she'd been kicked in the belly. For a moment she tried to believe it was a bad joke; either that or he'd been fooled. But it wasn't credible. Donovan had an odd sense of humour but he wouldn't joke about this. And to believe that about Shapiro he'd need overwhelming proof. She said quietly, 'Tell me what you've found out.'

If Shelley had taken the photograph himself it couldn't have disappeared into the black hole of Queen's Street in the way it did. But it wasn't taken by anyone local, it was sent to the *Courier* by a London street photographer who found that one of his customers had been accused of a celebrated crime.

'The nationals carried a couple of pars when Foot was charged and the snapper recognized the name and address. He didn't know it mattered if Foot was in London that particular day, he just thought he could make some money out of it. The nationals weren't interested so he sent it to Foot's local rag. But the *Courier* had shots of Foot coming out of their ears – every time Shelley went to a meeting or demonstration, there was Foot grinning at him from the front row – he didn't need to buy another. He was going to return it.'

Donovan broke his narrative long enough to drag on his coffee as if it were a cigarette. 'The court appearance was only a remand, Foot's defence didn't come into it.

But we were asking a lot of questions, and by now half the town knew he was claiming to have been in London with this girl Sue. Shelley thought we'd like to know that at least some of it was true: there was a girl, and Foot did get as far as London. He gave the print, and the snapper's name and address, to the Chief.'

Now Liz knew why Donovan had come here. The implications of this, for the inquiry and for Shapiro, were impossible to exaggerate. They had embarked on this exploit, or Donovan had embarked and she'd let him, in the certainty that once the source of the photograph was known Shapiro would be exonerated. They'd given no thought to the possibility that what they discovered might bury him.

Liz didn't want to think about it, not yet. She wanted to be sure she had the facts straight first. She wanted to be sure there'd been no mistake, on Donovan's part or Tom Shelley's, to explain the otherwise inexplicable. If she had to confront this she would, but only when she'd dismissed the easier options.

'Why did Shelley say nothing about it before now? For God's sake, he'd seen evidence that cast serious doubt on a major criminal conviction. Why did he do nothing for eight years? And what suddenly galvanized him now?'

The hot drink, or perhaps just talking, was helping Donovan to relax. The terrible tension of his steel-strung body was easing perceptibly, the black gravel in his voice that had made him almost incomprehensible beginning to lighten. Some of his pent-up breath left him in a sigh. 'A misunderstanding. Shelley assumed we were dealing with the guy who took the picture. And the snapper must have assumed the *Courier* weren't interested in buying it, and didn't bother asking for it back because the man who'd paid for it was in gaol with more on his mind than holiday pictures.'

'And when Foot was convicted?'

'Shelley supposed that the photograph wasn't significant after all. He didn't know if it was or not, he just thought it might be. When the Chief went ahead with the charges' – he shrugged awkwardly, like a damaged bird – 'Shelley assumed he'd looked into it and found it of no value. He never imagined for a moment that he'd just thrown it away.'

Liz's cheeks turned hot. She resisted the urge to shout at him but couldn't keep the venom out of her voice. 'We don't know that's what he did.'

'Don't we? You can think of another explanation?' He was disturbed in a way she'd never seen him before. She'd seen him angry often enough: angry enough to do stupid things like risking his career and his neck. She'd seen him right and she'd seen him wrong. She'd seen him battle against big battalions and personal ghosts. But she'd never seen him look so totally out of his depth before. He didn't know what to believe.

She made herself breathe calmly. 'All right. We've hit on something a bit surprising, that's all. There may be a perfectly good explanation. Maybe he did look into it and found it proved nothing. Maybe it was taken before those two days Foot was missing.'

Donovan shook his head stubbornly. 'He said he never saw a photograph, not that it wasn't relevant.' His voice creaked as if a little more pressure would crack it.

Liz tried to think. 'So maybe he made a mistake. An honest mistake, the kind we all make – I do, you do, the Chief must have made some in his time. Maybe he put the picture aside, meaning to find out about it, and – forgot—?' It sounded so lame she avoided looking at him.

'Forgot? Something that important? A man was dead, and another man was facing trial, and he forgot to check out an alibi?' Incredulity sent Donovan's voice soaring. 'Even if he did, wouldn't he have remembered the moment God mentioned a photograph? You would. You'd think, Christ Almighty, I never did check that out! You know the Chief, he's got a mind like a filing cabinet.

He doesn't lose things. And if he did, just that once, he wouldn't lie about it.'

'So what *are* you suggesting? That he deliberately concealed evidence to obtain a conviction?'

'No! But—' He couldn't find another explanation either.

'Could Tom Shelley be lying?'

That was the best they could hope for. Donovan shook his head. 'I don't see it. He didn't come to me, after all, I went to him. And why would he lie? What would he have to gain?'

'What would the Chief?' But that was obvious enough. If Shapiro had taken a short-cut eight years ago, under pressure to get a result and either believing Foot was guilty despite the photograph or despairing of convicting anyone else, then he'd have to lie about it. It wouldn't be the first time a policeman, even a senior policeman, had done something stupid and tried to lie his way out. She wouldn't have believed it of Frank Shapiro. But nor could she ignore the evidence.

'I'll talk to him,' she decided, the prospect like lead in her belly. 'There's no point telling God – he's got the photograph, he knows. But we got ourselves involved in this, I think we have to see it through. Maybe there's something we haven't thought of. The least we owe Frank's the chance to explain. If there is no explanation at least he'll know the shit's about to hit the fan.'

Donovan looked at her with respect. 'You might be better staying out of this. I'll go see him if you like.'

Liz shook her head. 'No. No offence, Donovan, but I don't want to put him in the position of having to confess to his sergeant. I don't know where this is going to end, but I'd like to keep it dignified as long as I can.'

'You'll let me know what happens?'

'Of course.'

7

Shapiro wasn't going to his office but he'd been up for hours when the soft purr of a car outside his house heralded a visitor. It wasn't rational but his mind shot straight to David. One more chance? he wondered. One more chance to squander?

But it wasn't David, it was Liz, and he knew from her expression that something had happened. He ushered her in, his eyes on her tight, controlled face, without quizzing her. Once the door was shut he opened his mouth to ask, but by then she was quizzing him and her eyes on his face were hard. He'd never seen them so hard.

'Why didn't you tell us the truth about the photograph?'

He stared at her, the helplessness of not understanding in the twist of his face and the way he fisted down the pockets of his fawn cardigan. '*What* photograph?'

She clung on to her patience, though there was little charity left in it. 'The photograph of Trevor Foot and the girl Sue. The one taken by a street photographer in London during the two days Foot was unaccounted for.' She breathed in and out once. 'The one Tom Shelley of the *Courier* gave you.'

The breath whispered out of him. 'You've seen it?'

Her jaw clenched on bitter disappointment. 'Did you think that after eight years it couldn't come back to haunt you? Oh, Frank, whatever were you thinking of?'

He realized with a shock that she'd misunderstood, and with a second and deeper shock that – perhaps for the first time – she wasn't assuming he had an explanation. Almost daily there were aspects of their working lives capable of misinterpretation. They knew better than to leap on such shadows as signs of bad faith. The least they owed one another was a hearing.

He said quietly, 'Liz, I'm going to say it once more, and after that it's up to you whether you believe it. I never saw a photograph of Foot and his girl. I wasn't shown a photograph by Tom Shelley or anyone else. Not when I was interviewing Foot, not afterwards and not since. The first I knew of any photograph was when God called me to his office and sent me on leave. I don't know why Shelley should lie about it – unless he and Foot were better friends than anyone knew – but he is doing. I don't remember talking to him about Foot; if I did he didn't give me anything useful. No information, and no photograph.'

Liz hesitated, confounded by his blanket denial. All her instincts were to trust him. But training and experience required her to weigh the facts. Of the two men, there was no doubt whom she preferred to believe. But only one of them had a reason to lie. She shook her head doubtfully. 'Donovan's talked to Shelley. He thought he was telling the truth.'

'You mean, he decided I was lying?' Shapiro wasn't shouting. In the cool centre of his brain where he could watch what was happening as if he were not involved he knew Liz was only doing her job – or if not her job, at least the one she'd taken on. But he couldn't keep a note of outrage, and a deeper one of personal hurt, out of his voice.

He'd never been in this position before. His career had been sound rather than meteoric, he lacked the glamour of a star player. But one thing he'd always been able to count on, so much so that at times he forgot how rare and important it was, was the respect of his colleagues. He felt the loss like a robbery, almost like a rape. It was a salutary experience. Even a week ago he wouldn't have

130

believed how much it hurt that his sergeant preferred to believe a newspaper photographer.

If he expected sympathy, what he got must have been a shocking disappointment. Liz was baffled, and upset, and knew that if Shapiro was lying ten years' worth of a relationship in which she'd invested at both personal and professional levels was a mirage. It would have been easy to back him right or wrong, and if she was wrong to throw herself on the mercy of a Force which, however much time it spent telling detectives to think for themselves, spent even longer telling them to obey their superiors. If she was wrong she was only like everyone else Shapiro had duped. If she was right she was his salvation. It was the safe option: to believe him until a superintendent or above ordered her to stop.

But she knew better than that. She wouldn't pay him lipservice, she had to be convinced. He had to earn her trust afresh. She snapped back at him, 'Don't try playing my heartstrings, Frank, I haven't got any. Donovan has. He'd walk through fire for you. He was taking a chance when he went to see Shelley. He wouldn't have believed that you suppressed evidence that could have cleared Foot if he'd had any choice. Now, can you suggest some way that Shelley could have given you that photograph and you could not have received it?'

A possibility, perhaps the only possibility, occurred to them simultaneously. Shapiro got it out first. 'He didn't give it me. He sent it me.'

'And it got lost in the post?' Liz's tone was hardly encouraging. Though she'd had the same thought she wasn't going to grab at it unless it offered more than a convenient way out.

Shapiro shook his head. 'He wouldn't post it. The *Courier*'s only round the corner – he'd hand it in at the front desk.'

'Without speaking to you? Without explaining where it came from?'

131

'Well, he didn't,' insisted Shapiro. 'Maybe I was out. Maybe he asked for me, and when I wasn't there he left a message.'

'Which the person who lost the photograph also forgot to pass on?'

'Doesn't sound too likely, does it?' he admitted ruefully. 'But something like that must have happened. Ask Shelley what he did – what he actually physically did – with the photograph.'

'I handed it in at the front desk,' said Shelley. 'I asked for Mr Shapiro but he wasn't in so I wrote a covering note and left it at the desk.'

'Mr Shapiro says he never received it.'

'Really?' Shelley's eyes bugged as he realized what that meant. 'You mean, nobody saw the photograph before Trevor Foot stood trial?'

Liz lifted one shoulder in half a shrug. 'Could be. We're not supposed to mislay evidence but anything's possible. Weren't you surprised that Mr Shapiro didn't call you about it?'

'I was a bit pissed off, yes. I assumed he'd contacted the snapper direct – I put his letter in with the picture – but I thought he could have let me know the outcome.'

'When was this?'

'A few days after Foot's first court appearance. It was the court report that gave the chap in London the idea of selling us the picture.'

'What was his name? Do you remember his address?'

'After eight years? When this was the only contact I ever had with him?'

'Have you any idea how I could find him?'

Shelley shook his head. 'Sorry, Inspector.'

Donovan had. 'If God's got the photograph he's probably got the letter as well.'

Liz stared at him. 'What are you suggesting?'

132

Donovan rocked his hand. 'I don't know. How much help would the letter be?'

'It would get us the man who's supposed to have seen Trevor Foot and this girl Sue in London at a time when he was supposed to be involved in the raid on BMT.'

'It could clear Foot of the charge he's doing time for.'

'Yes. If the photograph puts him in London at the time of the raid he's free and clear. If it puts him in London any time in the two days he was missing the case'll be reopened.'

'Won't do the Chief much good, though, will it?'

She saw no point in lying. 'None at all. Material evidence in the case went missing after Shelley handed it in with the Chief's name on it: the onus is on him to show he never received it. I don't know how he'd do that.'

'Do you still want to see the picture?'

She had no illusions about what he was asking or the likely consequences. Neither photograph nor photographer could disprove the allegation against Shapiro. But they could shine a light where they were currently groping blindly for the truth. The cost, to all of them, might be enormous. Foot, whether or not he did what he was imprisoned for, would soon be free anyway. Liz was considering staking her future, and Donovan's, and Shapiro's, merely to speed his release.

Or conceivably to find, once the wind was irretrievably sewn and the whirlwind already in the reaping, that the photograph contained no defence after all, that Foot was guilty as charged. Then she'd have done it for nothing.

'Yes,' she said.

8

Donovan always looked as if he was up to something. Partly it was the ectomorph outline, all length and no width and a slight stoop from keeping his hands in his pockets when they weren't in use. Partly it was his colouring, so dark as a result of ancestral Spanish infusion that it was traditionally described as Black Irish. In a large part it was due to personal mannerisms: the wariness of his gaze, the way he returned greetings – when he returned them – to a point just over people's right shoulders, and the way he mumbled when anyone asked what he was doing. He could look shifty fetching coffee from the canteen.

People new to Queen's Street tended to hear the accent, press alarm buttons and report an intruder acting suspiciously. People who knew him attached no significance to the fact that Sergeant Donovan constantly looked as if he was up to something he didn't want anyone else to know about.

This was a positive advantage when he was up to something he didn't want anyone else to know about.

Miss Tunstall, who had been Superintendent Taylor's secretary for longer than Donovan had been in Castlemere, only sighed wearily when he sidled round her door, fixed his eyes on her in-tray and mumbled, 'I've come for the photograph.'

'What photograph's that, Sergeant?'

Donovan's gaze slid off the desk and over the carpet to Taylor's door. He knew, of course, had made sure

134

before coming this far, that the Superintendent was out of the building. 'The one for the *Police Review*. Bob Cassidy's retirement party.'

Station Sergeant Cassidy had indeed retired, there had been a party and photographs had been taken. Since Cassidy had effectively run Castlemere for some fifteen years a photograph had undoubtedly been sent to the *Police Review*. But it wouldn't have come from Superintendent Taylor so Miss Tunstall would know nothing about it.

She frowned. 'He didn't say anything to me about it.'

Donovan shrugged. 'Supposed to leave it on his desk.'

'I'll go and look.' Used as she was to Donovan prowling round like a hungry wolf she suspected nothing when he followed her into Taylor's office.

There was no photograph in any of his trays – he had twice as many as normal mortals, station legend had it they were marked In, Out, Pending and Too Difficult – but by then Miss Tunstall was on her mettle, unwilling to admit defeat. Without prompting she opened the long shallow drawer above the knee-hole and went through the papers she found there with deft fingers. 'Is this—'

Donovan's fingers were pretty deft too: he had the stiffened envelope out of her hands before she knew he was reaching for it, and the flap open and the contents slid out while she finished the sentence. '—the one?'

He pushed the print, and the letter folded round it, inside the envelope again and handed it back. 'Nah,' he said negligently, 'that's just some feller and his bird.'

'Well, there doesn't seem to be anything else here,' said Miss Tunstall. 'I'll ask Mr Taylor when he gets in, shall I?'

'OK. No, wait a minute,' Donovan said then, 'I wonder if he left it at the front desk? I'll try there. If I don't track it down I'll come back when Sir's in.'

'Very well.' Miss Tunstall saw him out, and had no idea he'd already got what he'd come for.

He took the stairs two at a time, mumbling to himself

135

all the way. Even people who knew him thought he was getting odder. But he reached Liz's office with the name and address he'd read off the letterhead still clear in his mind. 'Mervyn Phipps, 23c DaSouza Buildings, Edgware Road,' he announced triumphantly as he shut the door behind him.

Liz's eyes gleamed. 'How on earth—? No, don't tell me. Will anyone suspect?'

'Shouldn't do. I doubt God's Rottweiler will even mention it, but if she does he'll just think I got it wrong. He always starts with that assumption anyway,' he added dourly.

Liz was regarding him speculatively. 'That stuff you're working on. Not exactly life and death, is it?'

'Not hardly.'

'Got your bike here?'

'Nowhere else to keep it.'

She looked out the window. 'I wonder how long it would take to ride to London and back.'

He understood perfectly. He always understood inferences: it was instructions he had difficulty with. 'Dunno. Listen, I've got an appointment at the dentist. I'll be back in a couple of hours.'

'Without breaking the speed limit,' added Liz obliquely.

Donovan gave his saturnine grin. 'In that case the dentist'll take a bit longer.'

Even on the motorway, with the speedometer sneaking over the limit, it took him well over an hour to reach the start of the Edgware Road. Donovan spent most of the time wondering what he'd tell Mervyn Phipps when the photographer asked why Superintendent Taylor had sent someone else to interview him. He thought he'd have to go carefully to get Phipps to repeat what he must already have told Taylor without revealing the fact that his enquiries were unauthorized.

In the event, though, that wasn't his problem. His prob-

136

lem was concealing his puzzlement when Phipps said testily, 'What photograph?'

He was a slim balding man in his early fifties who dressed as if the seventies had never reached the Edgware Road. He wore open-neck flower-printed shirts and flared jeans, and looked as if he'd produce a silver bell on a chain at the drop of a Beatle cap.

Donovan breathed heavily. 'Trevor Foot. Him and his girl: the one you sent to the *Castlemere Courier.*'

That rang a bell. 'Oh – the Beast of Castlemere. Jesus, that's going back a bit.'

'Eight years.' He frowned. 'But it's not eight years since you handled that photo, is it?'

'Yes.' A buzzer went off in the dark-room behind them. Phipps excused himself and came back a minute later drying his hands. 'What's this all about?'

Donovan was confused. 'Has nobody talked to you about this business in the last week?'

'No,' said Phipps. 'Who?'

'Well – us. Castlemere police. I thought I was following up an earlier contact.'

'Not with me, squire,' Phipps said with conviction. 'What about?'

The conversation was becoming surreal. Donovan shook his head to clear it. 'About the photograph,' he said, enunciating very clearly. 'The picture of Foot and his girl. That you took. That you sent to the *Courier.*'

'And Castlemere police want to talk about it after eight years? I've heard about delays in the justice system but that's ridiculous.'

'No. Yes,' said Donovan, by now totally flummoxed. 'I mean, we haven't had it for eight years. At least . . .' He drew a deep breath and started again. 'Didn't you send us a copy of it about a week ago?'

'Why would I do that?'

'So you didn't?'

'No. I haven't thought of the Beast of Castlemere since

– well, since eight years ago. I only sent the original to your local paper on the offchance, and they weren't interested enough to buy it. Or even return it, the sods. I haven't given it a thought from that day to this.'

'Well, *somebody* sent us a copy.'

'I doubt that, squire,' said Phipps. 'I've got the negative, I'd know if another copy had been printed.'

Donovan had no idea what all this meant, but he was damned if he'd come all this way for nothing. 'Well, can you print me a copy now?'

Phipps blew his cheeks out. 'I should be able to turn it up. When was it again?' Donovan gave him the date of the laboratory incident. Phipps opened a lower drawer in his filing cabinet.

'Can you say what time it was taken?' Donovan was looking ahead. If it was the day of the raid, it mattered whether it was first thing in the morning – giving Foot time to return to Castlemere – or late afternoon.

'Not to the hour. The date'll be on the receipt but they aren't timed. It just shows that people have paid. The system wasn't designed to provide alibis.'

He found the receipt without much difficulty. 'April the third. That any good to you?'

The raid occurred in the early evening of April 3rd. So far as anyone knew Foot had no transport of his own, which meant he couldn't put his foot down and be home in an hour and a half. If he was still in London in the afternoon it was unlikely he was at BMT at seven thirty.

'Can you tell from the other receipts what time of day it was?'

Phipps shook his head apologetically. 'Not really. April's not really peak time in this business. I only took a handful of orders after Foot, but that doesn't necessarily mean it was late in the day, it could just mean it was a rotten day generally. No way of telling.'

That made sense. Donovan had to fight down a quiver of relief that he mightn't after all get what he'd come for.

He was all too aware that, for once, finding the truth mightn't give him the golden glow of satisfaction. The truth this time might clear Foot, about whom he didn't give a toss, and incriminate a man he admired more than anyone alive. Not a lot of job satisfaction in that, he thought grimly.

But it didn't matter what he wanted. If Shapiro had offered his integrity as a hostage to fate – something Donovan still fought against believing however the evidence stacked up – his colleagues had no right to shield him from the consequences. Even if they wanted to.

'Can you make me that print?'

Phipps found the strip of negatives as easily as he'd found the receipt. 'Keep meaning to clear this lot out,' he said cheerfully. 'Good job I never got round to it.' He peered at it closely, sucked his teeth and set to work.

It doesn't take very long to print a negative once the equipment is set up. Donovan hung over the man's shoulder like a bird of ill omen, watching the ghost of an image beginning to form in the chemical bath. Slowly they became recognizable, the grinning man and the girl, arms around one another, posing cheesily for the camera.

'Camden Lock,' said Phipps judiciously, 'just up the road from the market.'

Donovan wasn't a Londoner. 'What would they be doing there?'

'Passing the time. It's got quite touristy, between the market and the canal development. There's cafés and craft shops and things. Spend a couple of hours no trouble. Oh, look.'

Donovan peered over his shoulder. 'What?'

'You wanted to know when I took it. Well, there's your answer.' It was a red and white striped van parked against the kerb in the background, with someone unloading bulky parcels on to the pavement. 'That's the evening papers arriving.'

'Oh, buggery,' said Donovan.

*

'I called at the shop, asked when they got their papers delivered. He said it varies a bit from day to day but it's always late afternoon. He couldn't remember them ever arriving before four.'

Liz sighed. 'So, while it may have been just physically possible, it would have been pretty difficult for Foot to do what he's in prison for. And now there's a photograph supporting his alibi. Oh, God, Donovan, this has got very messy.'

'I don't know where the photo came from,' said Donovan.

Liz blinked. Obviously, since he'd been talking to the man who took it, he didn't mean that. 'After so long, you mean.'

He nodded. 'Phipps says that until today he only ever printed the one copy. Foot paid for it and he was going to send it to him, but when he saw he was in custody he sent it to the *Courier* instead. That's the picture Tom Shelley received and left at the front desk for the Chief.'

'Well?'

'Well, what are we saying happened to it after that? If it reached the Chief and he decided to suppress it, he wouldn't leave it somewhere it could be found, he'd destroy it. And if he didn't receive it, where's it been these eight years that suddenly God's got it?'

'The bottom of his in-tray?' Liz hazarded.

Donovan gave her a quick grin before continuing. 'It makes no sense. It went AWOL either by accident or design. If it was deliberate, how come it's turned up again? If I've no choice I can just about believe in the Chief framing Foot; but dishonest *and* careless? No way. And if it just got mislaid, how come it stayed missing for eight years and *then* turned up?'

'What are you saying? That someone else mislaid it? Someone in this building? Who? Just suppose for a moment that the investigating team decided it was an embarrassment and they'd get rid of it. Can you see that decision coming from anyone but the man in charge? If it was deliberately disappeared it had to be Frank, and I don't believe that it was.'

They came from very different worlds. Liz grew up in the Vale of Evesham where the seminal image of summer was apple-blossom ripening into fruit under an azure dome. Some of the sun had entered her soul, and though she'd had to struggle for what she had achieved she'd been lucky too. She'd had to fight for acceptance in the male world of crime investigation. She'd been frustrated by the prejudice of senior officers who failed to recognize, precisely because it was so ubiquitous, the glass ceiling that broke the careers and spirits of so many talented women; and by the casual bigotry of junior colleagues who consistently under-valued women's potential at the sharp end of the job. That notwithstanding, she had always found allies in the Force, people like Shapiro willing her to succeed. She had earned the respect, grudging at times, of officers ranked both higher and lower than herself at each stage of her career, and the harvest of that was a confidence that allowed her the luxury of trusting people sometimes.

Her sergeant grew up in a gritty mid-Ulster village, its scant natural attractions turned to ashes and scattered down the wind by the small holocaust that began about the time Cal Donovan was learning to read from gable-ends. (The village school, in line with its strict non-partisan policy, had 'Brits Out' painted on one wall and 'No Pope Here' on another.) Though the sun must have shone on Glencurran occasionally it was a dark place by nature: squatting over a little peaty river in a fold of barren upland, it defined what Brussels meant by the phrase 'Less-Favoured Area'.

Something of that entrenched grimness touched its finger to its children's lips and Donovan carried the shadow of it folded in his own. Long after he'd left the place, even after he had no family tying him to it, he continued to see the world through Glencurran eyes. He expected nothing he hadn't fought for, mistrusted anything that came too easily, sought ulterior motives for everything. It made him an effective policeman but a difficult human being.

Because of the differences between them Donovan could look at the same things as Liz and see them differently. Even when, as now, his inability to accept the convenient made him deeply unhappy. Experience warned him that life wasn't cosy, it was brutal, and nothing that depended on a happy coincidence was likely to be true.

If it had been in his nature to compromise he'd have kept his counsel, hoped for the best, waited to see if this time his suspicions might prove groundless. But it wasn't and he couldn't. He shook his head stubbornly. 'And I don't believe that anything that convenient was an accident.'

9

It was no longer possible to keep their activities from Superintendent Taylor. A man had been in prison for eight years for an offence it was unlikely he'd committed: procedures had to be started to secure his release. That was only the beginning. There would be inquiries, reviews, the question of compensation. If it was messy now it would be shambolic before it was finished. But it had to be done. Taylor wasn't in his office so Liz phoned first then went to his home.

It was a difficult interview and Taylor made no effort to help her, sitting stony-faced while she explained how in effect she hadn't trusted him to investigate the allegation against DCI Shapiro so she'd sent Donovan to do it instead. That was the only place where she could have put a different gloss on it: she could have let him think Donovan did it on his own. It was almost the truth. But if God wanted somebody's head he'd find it harder to take Liz's, and it was also true that if the idea had been Donovan's the authority had been hers. She told him what they'd done and what they'd discovered.

Taylor heard her out in ominous silence. Then he said, 'I see. You expected to be able to disprove the allegation against Mr Shapiro, and instead you've found out that he secured a conviction against an innocent man. Tell me: how did you find the street photographer?'

Liz came out with perhaps the only lie she'd ever told a senior officer. 'Shelley remembered the name. We were able to trace him.' If anyone thought to ask, Shelley would deny it. She hoped no one would ask.

'And where do you suggest we go from here?'

'I suppose you call the Chief Constable and he sends someone from Complaints to interview Mr Shapiro. We will of course co-operate any way we can.'

'Even if that means throwing Mr Shapiro to the wolves?'

'This has gone way beyond personal loyalties, sir.'

Taylor nodded slowly. 'That at least is something we can agree on. Well, Inspector, I have some news for you. I have not, as you seem to think, been doing nothing. Now I know who did what I can tell you what happened. You'll be glad to learn that while I agree with you that Trevor Foot is innocent I don't believe that therefore Mr Shapiro is guilty.'

Finally he invited her to sit. 'I wanted to make sure none of this had been done to disguise something nasty. But it seems to have been nothing more than a tragic error: a moment's carelessness rather than premeditated malice. Somehow – we may never quite know how but you know how busy the front desk can get – the envelope Shelley left for DCI Shapiro got put aside instead of being sent to his office. Things got put on top of it, the whole pile got moved a few times, and that envelope ended up with a stack of other manila envelopes in the stationery drawer. If it had had Mr Shapiro's name on it it wouldn't have happened. But Shelley expected to hand it to him, it was only when he found he couldn't do that that he scribbled a covering note and put it in the envelope with the photograph. There was nothing written on the outside.

'So it sat there, year after year, always at the bottom of the drawer with new supplies going on top. But last week a requisition went missing so our stationery didn't turn up on time. I needed a stiffened envelope, took the last one, and the rest you can guess.'

Liz's eyes were wide with shock; her mouth had dropped open too. 'An accident? A simple straightforward terrible bloody accident! The picture got mislaid, and because of the precise combination of circumstances nobody knew to look for it. Nobody framed Foot, but he's still done eight years he didn't deserve. Dear God. What's the Chief going to say?'

Taylor's expression melted just a fraction. 'His first reaction will be relief that he's in the clear. Then he'll be glad we have only an act of criminal carelessness to explain and not something worse. After that he might be interested to hear how you reached the conclusion that he'd deliberately and with malice aforethought perverted the course of justice.'

Liz's eyes were beginning to ache. She closed them for a moment. 'I'm going to owe him an apology. I owe you one too.'

Taylor sniffed. 'Don't worry about that. You were wrong but you could have been right: you had to do something about it. When this breaks loose we'll have enough people after our blood without cutting one another's throats.'

'What do you want me to do?'

He walked her to the door. 'I don't see any need for you to get involved. Do your job. Very soon the Chief Constable'll know, the Press'll know and the Civil Rights lot'll be on to it. We're going to take a beating: me because a piece of vital evidence went missing in my station, Frank Shapiro because he put an innocent man in prison. Once the wolves gather you may be the only one who isn't under attack. I'll have to rely on you for all sorts of things. You could end up running the station.'

The prospect gave Liz no pleasure. 'And we've still got an arsonist on the loose, and only two days to catch him before the shopping centre opens.'

Taylor couldn't resist putting the boot in gently. 'You may be wrong about that. Any of us can make a mistake, Inspector, even you.'

145

She'd got off lightly and she knew it, she didn't begrudge him a little gentle sniping. 'I'm fully aware of that, sir. I'm just – very uneasy about it. I'll be glad when Monday's over.'

'I wish I thought my problems would be resolved so soon,' said Taylor, showing her out.

As she walked to her car the sudden acrid whiff of smoke curled under her nostrils and she spun in alarm. But it was only a gardener raking leaves on to a bonfire.

The tall young man watching from the conservatory door saw her searching wildly for the source of the smoke. He smiled. 'No arsonists here, Inspector. We're all hot and bothered, but that's our own fault for turning a family wedding into a three-ring circus.'

Robin walked her to her car. 'I hear David Shapiro's back.'

Something in the way he said it made her look at him. 'Do you know him?'

'We were all at school together – David, Alison and me. With our fathers working together it was rather assumed that we had more in common than we actually had.'

Liz said carefully, 'That could be an irritation.'

He shrugged easily. 'David's all right. Alison liked him well enough – I think he appealed to her maternal instinct though there's barely a year between them. I always found him – I don't know – a little odd somehow. A little tense. I think he found it hard measuring up to family expectations.'

Liz wasn't sure what he was telling her but she thought there was something. She didn't know David Shapiro, her only interest in his personal angst was its effect on her chief. But she also didn't know Robin Taylor so this wasn't just a casual conversation. 'He seems very determined to make a go of the photography.'

'Yes, he would be. He was always anxious to succeed in whatever he tackled. Or at least for people to think he'd succeeded.'

146

'Talking big? Isn't that par for the course with teenagers?'

'Oh yes,' agreed Robin. 'I'm sure he grew out of the other stuff a long time ago.'

This was it then: she saw it coming. 'Other stuff?'

'I never believed half of it anyway,' he said blithely. 'People exaggerate, don't they? Chemistry labs are always catching fire, it's their nature. If he'd really cooked up a Molotov cocktail, they'd never have let him finish the year.'

He may have intended to say more. Certainly there were things she wanted to ask. But just then somebody called his name and they turned to see the big man in the army pullover, whom Liz had taken for the gardener, striding towards them. Robin gave a quick dip of his head. 'I'll have to go now, my uncle's looking for me.' He backed away so smoothly that she might have imagined he'd been there beside her, speaking to her. After a moment she got in her car and drove back to town, slowly because she was thinking.

It sometimes seemed to Liz that the longer she knew Donovan the less she understood him. She thought he'd be ecstatic when she told him Shapiro was in the clear, that although something rather awful had happened it wasn't deliberate and it wasn't the chief's fault. But Donovan just perched there on the windowsill, arms folded, long legs crossed at the ankles, his narrow face expressionless, while she related everything that had passed between Superintendent Taylor and herself.

What had passed between Robin Taylor and her she was keeping to herself until she had thought a little more about it.

When she'd finished and Donovan still didn't say anything she snapped at him, exasperated. '*Now* what's the matter?'

His voice was guarded and faintly apologetic. He knew he was rocking a boat it was in everybody's interests to keep steady. 'I don't know. Something. Did you believe him?'

Liz stared. 'God? Of *course* I believed him. Don't you?'

'I don't know. It's still awfully convenient, isn't it?'

She'd have liked to throw him out, send him back to his burglaries and put his weasel doubt out of her mind. But the last year had taught her that his instinct was one of the more reliable things about Donovan. 'Convenient for whom?'

'For both of them. OK, there'll be a stink over it and it'll set God's OBE back a year, but it won't reflect on him as badly as his detective chief inspector framing someone.'

Unable to contain her resentment, Liz came to her feet and paced the room, throwing angry glances over her shoulder. 'Is that really what you think? That the Chief sent Trevor Foot to prison for eight years when he knew he was innocent, and that when he found out Superintendent Taylor risked his own career to protect him? Is that what you believe?'

Donovan's short fuse reached its explosive end. 'God damn it, I don't know what I believe! I've always thought the Chief was an honest man, I want to go on thinking that. But – I don't believe in coincidences; at least not convenient ones. I don't believe in vital evidence lurking at the bottom of a stationery drawer for eight years. And I don't believe that if God had found the photograph the way he said he'd have sent the Chief on leave while he looked into it. Why would he? He couldn't think Shapiro had hidden it there; if he'd wanted rid of it he'd have destroyed it.

'It stinks of cover-up. And I don't think Taylor would risk his pension covering up for you, or me or a careless desk sergeant or almost anyone else here. But he just might do it for a man who'd given him eight years' good work, who did something stupid just once.'

'Stupid? If he did what you think that wasn't stupid, it was criminal. Short of murder it's about the worst crime a policeman can commit. What has Frank Shapiro ever done to you that you think he's capable of that?'

Donovan shook his head, once, in anger and distress. 'Nothing! I mean . . .' He hadn't the words to say what he meant. 'For Christ's sake, I don't want to be right about this! Only, looking at the two of them, you can see how it could happen.'

Liz didn't understand. 'The Chief and God?'

'The Chief and Foot! Do I have to spell it out? The Chief's a Jew, isn't he? And Trevor Foot was too right-wing for the National Front.'

Then Liz understood what he was saying. Her eyes burned his face for a moment, then she turned away in disgust. 'You're sick, do you know that?'

'So what do you want me to do?' Donovan cried. 'Go along with it? Because I owe the Chief at least as much as you and Taylor do. For all the times he's spoken up for me, shouldn't I keep quiet for him? He's believed in me times when it took an effort of will like fire-walking. Times when it could have done him damage. Surely to Christ I owe him something in return?

'This? Tell me this is how I pay him back and I'll do it. Tell me it's more important to protect a man who's done as much good as Frank Shapiro than a little toe-rag like Trevor Foot, who'd probably be in prison for something else if he wasn't there for this, and I'll believe it. I'll do my damnedest to believe that. Only, it isn't what I've always thought. It isn't what I thought we were here for.'

Liz stared at him, amazed. The strength of his passion, the depth of his feeling and the intimate way he was in contact with it, reaching down into the heart of himself with bloody shaking hands, both startled and moved her. She was not herself an emotional person. Her strengths were the cerebral ones of clarity, judgement, perception. These were the tools with which she had shaped her personal and professional lives, and for the most part she was content with the result. She had a comfortable relationship with her husband, an easy one with colleagues, a job that gave her challenge and satisfaction and a kind of amused tolerance for hotter-blooded souls whose emotions got them into trouble.

But for a split second, watching a young man rip himself apart in front of her, Liz Graham wished there was something she wanted as much as Donovan wanted not to be Frank Shapiro's Nemesis.

After a moment she blinked and swallowed. He'd racked himself in front of her, and it was hard to go on talking with that livid in her mind. But he was waiting for a reply, his eyes molten on her face.

She fell back on the calm that had served her in the past, though this time she was simulating a detachment she didn't feel. She said quietly, 'I'm not going to say that. Of course I'm not. I hope you're wrong about this, but if you're right then no, it makes no difference who Frank is and what he's done since he did this. Or only to us, not to what we do about it.

'Listen, Donovan. The wheels are in motion, Foot'll soon be free. That takes the urgency out of it. Wait a few days, see what happens. Maybe once the Chief's back you'll feel differently. If not, if you still think there's been a deliberate perversion of justice, well, then you have to decide what you want to do about it. If you want to go on the record. It's a hell of a thing, but you don't need me to tell you that. If you're wrong you won't be able to go on working here.

'If I thought you were right I'd back you. I don't know if you believe that, but I would. Even if it meant us collecting our cards together. But I don't. I don't believe Frank Shapiro would do it, whatever the provocation. So unless you can produce some serious evidence you're on your own. Before you go any further, be sure you know what the consequences are likely to be. Right or wrong, you could lose everything.'

She left him to think about that. As she passed him,

heading for the corridor, she folded a tissue into his hand. 'There's something in your eye.'

He didn't know what she meant. But when she was gone and he raised an exploratory finger it met the damp of tears.

III

1

Liz put the Foot case out of her mind, was glad to do it. It was Sunday now: tomorrow night Castle Mall would welcome the public with a fanfare of marching bands and fireworks, and she remained convinced that the man with flames in his eyes would be among the crowds unless she could find him first.

Though she was reluctant to add further to Shapiro's problems, she knew she'd have to check what Robin Taylor had told her. But, at least in the first instance, she could do it discreetly. Brian could give her the information she needed. 'Who's head of the science department at Castle High?'

He stared at her over the breakfast table. 'Bill Freeman. For Heaven's sake, why?'

She didn't want to explain, even to him. 'How long's he been there?'

'Two or three years: something like that.'

'That's no good. I need to talk to someone who's been in the science department for six years or more.'

'There's Big Mac. She was Head of Science before she got the headship.'

Liz had met Mary McKenna on a handful of occasions in the year Brian had worked for her. The first was a 'Meet the Spouses' evening when Liz had gone determined to play the supportive housewife and ended up describing the factors governing the decomposition rates of corpses. She thought there was every chance Ms McKenna would remember her. 'Do you have her home number?'

He had. 'But she's probably in her office. She's usually there Sunday mornings, she reckons running a school would be easy without all the pupils and teachers getting in the way.'

She called first to make sure, then she went round. Ms McKenna met her at the side door. 'How can I help?'

McKenna remembered the fire in the chemistry lab. It had been her job to deal with the insurance, and the police. 'It wasn't the first fire I ever had, and it wasn't the worst. They're all nasty until they're under control. There's a lot of stuff in a lab that shouldn't be exposed to a naked flame.' She chuckled. 'It's our own fault, really. The first thing we do in chemistry is set fire to different substances and get the kids to describe what they see. It captures their imagination. There's always the risk of one of them getting too imaginative.'

Liz was all ears. 'You mean, one of the kids started it deliberately?'

McKenna was cautious. 'Do you want what I think or what I know?'

'Let's start with what you know.'

'There was a fire,' enumerated the Principal. 'The Fire Brigade reckoned it started about the end of the school day though it wasn't spotted until an hour later. It was confined to the chemistry lab. There was a lot of smoke damage, and the bench where it started – apparently in the cupboard under the sink – was a write-off. No one was hurt.'

'All right,' said Liz. 'Now what you think.'

'We all thought it couldn't have started spontaneously. There was no power supply to the bench so it wasn't that. The gas was off at the mains, and the only one who might have got away with having a quiet cigarette at the end of the day was me and I don't smoke. I had the last class of the day in there. When the bell rang I packed them off and locked up, and went to a staff meeting. We were still

156

talking when someone raised the alarm. I don't see how it could have been an accident. I think one of the little sods left a fire-bomb.'

Liz's eyes widened. 'Is bomb making on the curriculum?'

McKenna laughed. 'Hardly. The average teenage boy is enough of a menace to society without knowing how to make an incendiary device. But you don't need an M.Sc. to rig something simple. Like a stub of candle burning in a saucer of petrol: when the wax burns down there's a flash and anything combustible within a metre or so will flare up. I don't know if that's how it was done, but that would work and so would half a dozen other devices well within the scope of a chemistry student. He could have done it while I was in the room. You can't watch them every second, and even if I'd seen one of them with his head in the cupboard I'd have assumed he was putting equipment away.'

'Did you see anyone in the cupboard under the sink?'

'Your chief asked me that at the time. I couldn't remember then, and that was six years ago. Those cupboards are in constant use, it just wouldn't have registered.'

'All right. So there was no evidence but you thought it was probably one of the boys. A prank that got out of hand?'

'Let's be generous,' McKenna sniffed, 'and say so.'

'Did you suspect anyone in particular?'

'I had no reason to suspect anyone in particular,' the Principal answered obliquely. 'No one was ever accused.'

Liz recognized that as an evasion. 'But one name suggested itself above the others. A boy in that last class of the day?'

McKenna regarded her speculatively. 'Inspector, why do I get the feeling you know as much about this as I do? Ah,' she said then, as if understanding had dawned. 'Well, of course, I had to tell him what I was thinking: that the lad had been in trouble before, even though it hadn't come to anything it was enough to make us wonder. I know I embarrassed him but he was the investigating officer, it really wasn't an occasion for tact. If he'd ever shown his face on parents' night, maybe I could have put him wise before his son was prime suspect in an arson case.'

Shapiro also spent Sunday morning in his office, studying everything Liz had collected on the fires. There was less than he'd hoped for. Forensics had been of limited assistance, the trail of the oil can petering out somewhere between its being discarded by Ted Burton and picked up by the man with a different hobby. The DCI put his head round Liz's door in case she could add anything, but she wasn't there.

Then Superintendent Taylor called to say they both had an appointment with the Chief Constable, to be followed by a brief press conference. He might like to be thinking what he'd say if invited to comment.

Before he left the building he summoned Donovan. 'You're still looking for missing VCRs, yes?'

Donovan nodded warily. 'Nobody's told me different.'

'Right. Well, if you're off the arson inquiry I have a job for you. The Foot case.'

He wasn't expecting that. The mask of detachment veiling his eyes slipped for a moment. 'Foot's innocent, for God's sake! He couldn't have done what you said he did.'

'Do you think I don't know that?' Shapiro's voice was savage. 'Do you think I don't know that an innocent man's been in prison for eight years because I thought he was lying when he wasn't? Eight years, Sergeant. You think I'm bothered by what the Chief Constable's going to say? By what the Press are going to say? I made an assumption that cost another human being eight years of his life. Do you think that anything *anyone* has to say can make me feel worse about that?'

Donovan swayed under his vehemence as if his face

158

had been slapped. He desperately wanted to believe that Shapiro's distress was genuine. But he worried that the explanation offered was both too pat and too improbable to be true, in which case Shapiro was still lying. Donovan deeply resented being lied to.

'Then what do you want me to do? I don't understand.'

Shapiro was used to a certain truculence from his sergeant, but not to having it directed at him. 'Come on, Donovan, get your head together. If Foot wasn't at BMT, somebody else was. Several people, in fact, and I want them.'

'You always knew there were others,' objected Donovan. 'If you couldn't find them then, what makes you think I can find them now?'

'I was dealing with students who were high on principles and low on responsibility. Eight years on those same young men are going to have good jobs, families, a different perspective. Start with the darts players, their names and addresses are in the file. Go and see them, tell them what's happened. Eight years ago they were covering for someone whose ideals they sympathized with. They approved of bombing a vivisection lab, reckoned it was just bad luck that a nightwatchman got hurt.

'Well, maybe what happened to Stan Belshaw was an accident. But what happened to Trevor Foot was cold blooded and deliberate. The people on that raid knew that he wasn't there, they could have cleared him at any time, without even putting themselves at risk. But it suited them for me to be chasing the wrong damn fox. They knew Foot couldn't give them away, so as long as I concentrated on him they were safe. They let him go to prison rather than tell me that I'd got the wrong man. That was unforgiveable. With luck, one of the darts players will think so too. They may not have known who organized the raid or who was on it, but they knew who asked them to create a diversion at BMT. Get that name and we're in business.'

'What if they're worried for their own skins?'

'I can't promise immunity if that's what you mean. But you can tell them that I'm not looking to charge them. They were only ever involved on the periphery: until now they probably thought Foot *was* there. We could do them for obstruction, I suppose, but this long after it's hard to see any great public benefit in it. It would be my view that if they co-operate now we should consider their obligation discharged.' He sniffed. 'Perhaps you shouldn't mention that my view may not carry much weight after today.'

Donovan regarded him in silence, his expression hardly flickering. Then he said, 'It isn't a resigning matter. Not if it happened how you say. You didn't send Foot to gaol, a jury did. On the basis of all the evidence that reached you he looked guilty: you thought so, they thought so. They can't make you resign for that.'

'No, they can't sack me for that,' Shapiro agreed wearily. 'It was an honest mistake. But it cost too much. If you're in a position to deprive people of whole chunks of their lives, you don't make mistakes, even honest ones. It's a question of professional competence. You wouldn't employ an epileptic pilot and you shouldn't employ a detective chief inspector who can't recognize the truth when he hears it.'

'You're serious? You're going to chuck it over this?'

The ambivalence in his inflection troubled Shapiro. He had expected shock, anger, indignation: what he got was the steely precision of someone who wanted to be absolutely sure he had the facts straight. But reacting oddly was Donovan's stock-in-trade, it didn't have to mean anything. Shapiro sighed. 'At my age it's called early retirement.'

'It'll look like an admission of guilt.'

That put the spark back into Shapiro's eyes and the edge back on his voice. 'Well, maybe to you it will, Donovan. Fortunately, the people who've been in this business long enough to learn a bit about it will recognize it as the honourable thing to do. But I'm wasting my time, aren't I, talking to you about honour?'

160

It was not only a cheap shot, it was wide of the mark. Often, as now, it was Donovan's very personal sense of honour that made him difficult. Recognizing that, belatedly Shapiro began to apologize. 'I'm sorry, lad, I didn't mean—'

But Donovan's eyes flared at him, hot like a cornered animal's; then he turned on his heel and left without further comment.

Only after he'd gone did Shapiro catch the echo of something he'd said earlier. He frowned. '*If* it happened how I said?'

2

Shapiro was leaving with Taylor as she parked in the yard so Liz knew she didn't have to face him yet. The queasy little flutter of relief under her breastbone gave her no pleasure. She'd have to talk to him sooner or later, and better before she interviewed his son than after.

Assuming that she had to. The possibility could not be discounted that she'd got this wrong: made one leap of intuition too many. She'd have a better idea after talking to Donovan, who could also be relied on to keep it to himself if she was wrong. That would be the best outcome: if Donovan could tell her that David Shapiro wasn't out of his sight long enough to have started the fire at the timberyard.

She found him in the collator's office copying addresses off the computer screen, blinked at the heading on the file. '*Now* what?'

His eyes were sullen. 'Not my idea, boss. The Chief wants me to find out who did what Foot didn't. He seems to think it'll be easier now than eight years ago.'

Liz forbore to comment. Privately she thought both men were losing their grip, and she had her doubts about God. 'Tell me again about the fire at the wharf. You were on the boat: were you asleep?'

'Yeah, it was late.'

'What woke you up? The flames, the noise?'

'David woke me. I suppose the noise woke him.'

162

'What was he doing – staring out the window, climbing into his clothes?'

'I think he was already on deck. He shouted through the hatch, then he came below to make sure.' When he realized what it was she was asking his eyes sharpened and his voice dropped a note. 'He was dressed and he had his camera round his neck.'

They regarded one another in silence, fully aware of where this line of reasoning was taking them. They'd got Frank Shapiro against a wall and now they were proposing to put the boot in. Very quietly Liz said, 'Can you think of any reason David Shapiro *couldn't* have started the fire at Evanses?'

Donovan couldn't. 'But why would he? For kicks?'

'Kicks is the reason with any pyromaniac,' said Liz. 'Whoever did this it was for kicks. But actually David has another reason. His portfolio. He needs photographs like that to get the kind of job that'll involve taking more photographs like that. It's a self-rewarding strategy for him. If it comes off he may never have to start his own fires again.'

Donovan was catching up fast. 'The earlier fires – Rachid's and the warehouse. I don't know if David was in town on Friday last but he was certainly here on the Saturday: that's when he went to see Payne only Payne got rid of him.'

'He could have come down the previous day.' They were kicking the idea between them like footballers warming up. They weren't committed to it yet, but the longer it stayed in play the likelier it started to look. 'Did you know David was suspected of starting a fire at Castle High? About six years ago, in his last term there. And that Frank was told about this?'

Donovan's eyes were doing sums. 'It must have been about then his marriage broke up. He and Mrs Shapiro separated, and David went with his mother.' He looked up at her. '*Another* frigging coincidence?'

'It could be,' insisted Liz. 'For God's sake let's keep a grip on this. It's a theory, that's all, just a bit of kite flying. All the same, you could read it that way, couldn't you? David did something Shapiro couldn't forgive. All right, he got away with it, but they knew at the school and Frank knew. He was a detective chief inspector, and his son was relieving his teenage angst by setting fire to public property. There was an almighty bust-up: maybe Frank threatened to nick him, maybe the boy threatened to run away. Either way Angela had had enough. She walked out, and David went with her.

'He finished school, then Angela packed him off to college in – Brighton, was it? – a decent distance from both his father and his school, hoping he could make a fresh start where nobody knew. And maybe he did. Maybe the change of scene, and doing something he enjoyed, and getting away from the friction at home, helped him settle down.

'Until he found himself back here, debating whether to go and see his father which he didn't want to do because he knew they'd only argue again. The closer he got to that confrontation, the more he teetered on the edge. Maybe he still reacts to stress by wanting to set fire to things. He'd know Frank would investigate. Maybe that made it more compelling. Not only was he relieving his feelings, not only was he going to get some terrific photographs, he was striking out at his father as well. He was saying, "I can make a fool of you when you don't even know I'm here. And if you did you couldn't do a thing about it without admitting that you knew I did it once before." You've talked to David: does that sound possible to you?'

Donovan thought about it, his head tipped back, his face twisted by the narrowing of one eye. 'I don't know,' he said at last. 'I wouldn't say it was impossible. He's a strange one, the same lad – I mean, I can see him voting Liberal Democrat and joining Amnesty International, but

164

fire-raising? I don't know. Are we sure about the incident at the school?'

'It wasn't told to me as proven fact,' admitted Liz, 'but Ms McKenna thinks it's what happened. That's what she told Frank.'

'And he covered up for the boy.'

'That isn't fair. There wasn't any evidence it was David, only that it could have been. No one could have been charged on that basis. If Frank hadn't investigated the fire probably no names would have been mentioned: I think Ms McKenna was tipping off a parent rather than making an accusation.' But Donovan was still troubled. 'Why, what are you thinking?'

He gave an unhappy shrug. 'A week ago I'd have said I knew the Chief pretty well. Now suddenly all sorts of stuff's crawling out of the woodwork and I don't know what I think any more. Was it only a mistake over Foot, or did he send him down because he needed a result and there was no one else handy? Was David entitled to the benefit of the doubt, or did the Chief use his position as investigating officer to lose evidence on that too? And if he did that, and even if he didn't, shouldn't it have struck him as suspicious when he saw David at the warehouse on Tuesday morning?

'So why didn't he do something about it? Even if he didn't know for sure, even if it was only a suspicion at the back of his mind, why didn't he say something? Instead of letting us chase round the countryside in search of Pakistani conspirators and oil cans from Manchester. Can you honestly say it still doesn't smell to you like a cover-up?'

'It's a completely different case,' Liz objected weakly.

'But it's the same man. The best reason for not believing Shapiro threw Foot to the wolves was that nobody'd ever known him do anything shady before. That's no longer the position.'

'Two suspicions don't add up to proof,' she insisted.

'My grandad had a saying, too,' Donovan said grimly. 'You know, the one worked with the racehorses? He used to say, The first time a horse kicks you it's his fault. The second time it's yours.'

Of the darts players, one was no longer known at his former address, one was working abroad, one had died in a road accident and two were working in London though they still had parents in Castlemere. Only one was still living at the address he'd given following the incident at BMT, so Donovan started with him.

Keith Baker would have appreciated the elder Donovan's advice: he was a vet. After graduating he spent three years with a large-animal practice near Newmarket. Then he returned to Castlemere as junior partner to a local man who was beginning to find wrestling with bullocks hard work and preferred things he could put on a table.

As well as being the handiest of the darts players, Baker had the greatest potential as a supergrass. He was living and working in his home town, which made him more vulnerable to local opinion than someone living in the anonymous suburbs of a city. He was a professional man whose reputation was of fiscal as well as personal value to him. And he lived with his mother, a breeder of Welsh mountain ponies and a justice of the peace known to Castlemere's legal fraternity as Birch-the-Bastards Baker. Donovan could imagine young Keith resisting the full weight of the law for a principle he believed in but still crumbling in the face of maternal disfavour.

He arranged to meet Baker at the surgery. He had to wait: an equine colic took precedence. Then he had to wait a little longer while Baker cleaned and plastered two deep punctures in his forearm.

Donovan frowned. 'A horse did that?'

'Family dog,' Baker explained cheerfully. He was a

bulky young man with straw-coloured hair and a touch of the wind in his complexion that would be a full-blown ruddiness by the time he was forty. 'You're not best placed to defend yourself when you've got the other arm shoved up a horse's bum.' He grinned. 'I'll get my own back when it comes in for its vaccinations.'

Quite clearly the vet had no idea why a policeman wanted to see him, or even a vague anxiety about it. If he'd read about the Foot case being reopened he hadn't recognized its significance to him. It was a long time ago and he'd been a very young man, and he'd taken comfort from the fact that the man who died was defending premises that routinely tortured living creatures and the man who went to prison knew what he was risking when he volunteered. There's a shocking ruthlessness to youth. But Baker had grown up since then.

Donovan was in no mood for word-play, and he wasn't very good at it even when he was. He came straight to the point. 'Do you remember Trevor Foot?'

For a moment Baker didn't. Donovan saw him puzzling over the faint bell the name rang. When recollection came Baker's eyes flared for an instant before shutters dropped behind them. He said with infinite care, 'I never met him.'

'I know that,' growled Donovan. 'No one involved in that pantomime did.'

A lexicon of expressions was flitting across Keith Baker's open face as he wondered how much he dared say, what he dared ask. Still he opted for caution. 'I wouldn't know. I wasn't on the raid.'

'Yeah, that's right,' said Donovan, not troubling to keep the sneer out of his voice. 'You were just passing. You heard nothing, saw nothing, know nothing, right?'

'That's right,' agreed Baker softly.

'Then this will only be of academic interest to you. But Trevor Foot, who also claimed that he wasn't there and didn't hear, see or know anything, was telling the truth. It didn't do him any good, nobody believed him and he's

167

been in jail for the last eight years. But somebody knew he wasn't involved. The guy who set it up. Who organized the raid and laid on the diversion. He let Trevor Foot go to prison for eight years for something he knew he had no part in, and he never said a word. Not to us, not to the papers, not to anyone.'

There was a pause while Baker took it in, the burden of those eight years falling through his eyes. But he was a man who made important, even vital decisions on a daily basis and he wasn't going to be hustled into making a bad one for himself. He said slowly, 'How is it you think I can help you?'

Donovan took a deep breath. 'Mr Baker, I'll be straight with you. There was a time you'd have faced charges, if anyone had been able to prove you'd done what they thought you'd done. That time is past. We have a mess to clear up and we need help to do it.

'What do I want from you? A name. Not necessarily the man – or maybe it was a woman – who should have gone to gaol instead of Foot, though that would be best of all. Maybe the only name you know is the guy who organized the diversion, and maybe he wasn't much closer to the heart of events than you were. But somebody asked him to do that, and told him where to go and when, and that's who I want. He caused one man's death and ruined another man's life, and I don't know what kind of a Utopia you thought you were building that meant destroying people to make a point.'

Donovan had a certain crude skill as an orator, and if he tended to be stronger on passion than logic that did not lessen the strength of his appeal. He could occasionally move people far beyond anywhere they wanted to go by the sheer power of convictions which, even when suspect, were always intense.

Keith Baker found himself swaying under the onslaught. If it was true that he now risked very little by speaking out, it was also the case that he had nothing to gain. The episode was ancient history, he hadn't thought of it for years. He was a different man: older, wiser, certainly more cautious. He'd entered into the conspiracy – because that was what it was, they'd all known what they were doing – in a spirit of righteous indignation levened by sheer devilry. They had been outraged by the television coverage of a man they considered a moral bankrupt: their response had seemed absolutely justified. The destruction of the BMT laboratory hadn't cost Baker a moment's sleep.

When they learned that the nightwatchman was in hospital, and later that he'd died, a lot of the satisfaction went. They didn't feel responsible – they couldn't have known that he'd return to the burning building, let alone that he was an asthmatic – but nor did they do much celebrating after that. They didn't break ranks under the pressure of police questioning because they knew they could protect themselves and each other by staying silent. And they still believed that what they had done had needed doing.

It all looked a little different from where Baker stood now. If he could believe this policeman, the pressure was off as far as protecting himself and his friends was concerned. And he'd long ago come to terms with the fact of a man's death as a result of what they had done. It was something he regretted, deeply but not bitterly: he still felt that it was an accident in every way that mattered.

But the fate of Trevor Foot disturbed him. This was the first indication he'd had that Foot wasn't guilty as charged. Baker and his friends weren't involved in BEAST, its meetings and machinations, didn't know the names or faces of those who were. He had assumed that Foot was one of them, just a little less clever or less lucky than those who escaped scot-free. Baker had been sorry for him in the way he'd been sorry for the security man, in principle but without personal grief.

But if Foot was a scapegoat, everything was altered.

169

Baker couldn't have known Foot was going down for something he had no part of, but every member of BEAST knew. And none of them had spoken out. Not anonymously, not through channels designed to protect their secrecy; not at all. Not in eight years. Keith Baker was a decent man, a caring man; he didn't like to think of anything suffering needlessly. The vivisection of Trevor Foot started a slow anger in him.

He said quietly, 'I didn't know he wasn't one of them.'

'I thought that.' Donovan went on waiting.

Baker reached a decision. 'I won't tell you who called me. He wouldn't have known who was and wasn't on that raid any more than I did. But we knew who ran BEAST. We didn't turn him in because we supported what he was doing. But not this. You're telling me he sacrificed an innocent man. I don't know if he was on the raid, but it was his idea and he planned it. He could have told you Foot wasn't there.'

'Who?'

'They called him Red Kenny. He was doing postgraduate research in zoology, he knew all the facilities that used animals, what they used them for and what they did to them. He was a cocky bastard even then but we admired him for having the guts to tackle something many of us considered indefensible.'

He sighed. 'I mean, I'm a scientist. I'd find it hard to say that animals should never be used for experimentation of any kind. I'd have to set their misery against progress in human and veterinary medicine that wouldn't have happened any other way. An awful lot of dogs died in the study of diabetes, for instance, but a lot of people's kids died until it was done.' His lip curled then and his voice hardened. 'But I'm damned if I can see that it's worth blinding one rabbit to provide the world with water-proof mascara.'

Donovan let him finish. He didn't want to risk losing him now. Then he said, 'Red Kenny. Did you know his real name?'

170

Baker blinked. 'Yes, of course. Sorry – there's no way you'd know. But you'll have seen him too, at least on TV. Keaton Payne, the naturalist. He lives in Castlemere – up behind the spinney, Hunter's Lane I think. Now he's got his own show and publishers fighting for his latest book, and there are kids up and down the country wearing stickers showing Keaton Payne and a badger. Eight years ago he was Red Kenny, scourge of the vivisectors, leader of what was at least arguably a terrorist organization. And in my modest way I helped him.'

'Eight years ago,' growled Donovan, 'he let a pathetic little man go to prison for him. I bet if Trevor Foot ever joined the Keaton Payne Fan Club he'll let his membership lapse now.'

3

In the endemic violence of the inner-city ghettos, where the shape of the day is dictated by such things as peak drug-dealing and optimum car-stealing times, dawn is about the only part of the twenty-four hours when most people will be where they're supposed to be. Some of them will not get home until three in the morning; some of them will be out wheeling and dealing before eight. But between five and six a.m. the only people who aren't in their own beds are in other people's. In the inner cities a dawn raid means exactly that.

In provincial towns like Castlemere even the criminals tend to keep office hours, and a dawn raid at seven o'clock is early enough for most purposes. But Keaton Payne was a naturalist specializing in nocturnal wildlife, and the cars sent to collect him and his guest missed them by a good half-hour.

Liz had no one but herself to blame. She knew what Payne did for a living, should have realized that like the animals he studied he would be at his most active in the twilight hours. 'Damn.'

'Do you want us to go look for them?' asked Donovan. 'If we can find the Range Rover they won't be far away.' He'd roused a neighbour to ask what Payne drove. There was no sign of the vehicle at the house but David's van was parked at the back. So they'd driven off together, still pursuing the ideal image for this celebration of one of the country's great and good. The environmentally friendly

172

phoenix risen from the ashes of Red Kenny the BEAST.

Liz would have preferred to do this without a dragnet. The man she was here to arrest, whom she had reason to believe had committed a serious crime, would keep. There was no question of him either repeating the offence or skipping the country. Wrong metaphor, she thought parenthetically, with a little grin that none of those around her understood; a badger expert wishing to evade justice would undoubtedly go to ground.

But the man with him, against whom the evidence was highly circumstantial, and about whom she needed to talk to her superintendent since she couldn't expect an unbiased opinion from her chief inspector, could present a very real and immediate danger to a lot of people. If David Shapiro had done what she was afraid he'd done, he had to be taken out of circulation before Castle Mall opened with a bang this evening. Presumably he'd return for his van before then: she could mount a watch on Payne's house. But if she was wrong about David, arresting him wouldn't prevent an attack on the Mall. She needed time to discover whether he was responsible or not.

'Yes,' she decided. 'Find the car and bring them in. Keep it vague: let David think we want to talk to him about Payne. If at all possible I'd like still to be on speaking terms with Mr Shapiro when we've finished. One thing before you go. Open this van, will you?'

Anyone there could have done it with a simple toolkit and minimal damage. Donovan did it with the contents of his pockets and there was no sign it had been tampered with.

Inside was an incredible assortment of jumble. There were substances that could have been used to make a fire but nothing that couldn't be explained by the owner's profession. There was a faint smell of petrol: they tracked it down to a rag. There were no partly assembled incendiary devices or anything else conclusive. 'Gut feeling?' asked Liz.

173

'My gut feeling,' said Donovan carefully, 'is that I'm glad it isn't my decision.'

'Thanks a bunch,' Liz said sourly. 'Go find yourself a Range Rover.'

By the time she arrived back at Queen's Street, Taylor and Shapiro were in their respective offices. There was a message at the desk to see Shapiro as soon as she came in. She knew why, of course: he wanted to know why his entire department was engaged on a dawn raid he knew nothing about. 'Sorry, Frank,' she murmured, heading for the Superintendent's office.

She outlined the case she had against Payne, and Taylor nodded with satisfaction. 'That'll take some of the heat out of the situation, if we can say we're about to charge someone in connection with the Foot affair. Can I say that? How sure are you?'

'Pretty sure,' said Liz. 'Baker had no reason to lie. He could have been wrong, I suppose, but he said they all knew. I think it'll stick.'

There was a genuine warmth in Taylor's eyes. 'Good. Good work. Frank'll be pleased.'

Liz bit her lip. 'Well, yes. But less so about the other suspect I want to question.' She told him all she knew about David Shapiro, enumerating meticulously the strengths and weaknesses of all the fragments she'd got together. 'I wish it was clearer. If I was sure it was David I could stop worrying about tonight. I'm not that sure, but there's too much to ignore. In view of the circumstances – let's be honest, I mean because of who he is – I want your approval to question him.'

Taylor was staring at her as if she'd sought approval to take CID on a staff outing to the Isle of Wight. She refrained from prompting him. She'd spelled it out as clearly as she could, now she was awaiting instructions. It was one of those decisions he was paid to take.

He blinked the amazement out of his eyes and caught

174

his breath. 'Oh, God, what a mess. Does Frank know about this?'

'Not yet, sir, no. He'll have to if we question the boy.' She went on waiting.

Taylor drummed square well-manicured fingertips in thoughtful arpeggios on the polished surface of his desk: literally playing for time. 'Children,' he said then, the word bursting from him in a soft explosion. 'They break your heart so many different ways. Just when you think you've made it, you've brought them up, and everything's settled and sorted out, they spring something like this on you.' He glanced at her quickly, gave a faintly desperate little snort of amusement. 'We're in the throes of a family wedding,' he explained. 'It makes one reflective.'

Liz offered a sympathetic smile but no comment.

'Very well,' he decided. 'I don't think we have any choice. That amount of circumstantial evidence against anyone else we'd have to take seriously: it can't alter anything that he's Frank's son. Maybe if he'd been at home, so Frank could vouch for his activities. But the fact is Frank has no more idea what the boy's been up to than we have. No, we can't soft-pedal on this. If you're wrong it'll be a matter of fulsome apologies all round, and if Frank wants to sulk he'll have to. But if there's any chance that we can prevent an incident at the Mall tonight by bringing him in, that's what we have to do. And as soon as possible. Bring them in, the pair of them, and let's see what they have to say for themselves.'

'What do we tell Mr Shapiro?'

Taylor's beard went lopsided as he sucked on the inside of his cheek. 'We'll have to warn him. Naturally he'll be shocked. I don't want him also to feel we did this behind his back.'

'Shall I talk to him or will you?'

The Superintendent regarded her shrewdly. 'Easier for you if I tell him; but perhaps easier for Frank if you do.'

Liz nodded ruefully. 'There was a message for me to

175

see him when I came in. I'll go and break the glad tidings now.'

They found Payne's car in the little scenic park overlooking the watermeadows of the River Arrow. There were two figures on the river-bank half a kilometre away. Donovan waded down to them through knee-high corn ripe for the harvest.

When he was close enough to see their faces he thought it odd that David, who knew him, should look surprised and Payne, who did not, should look at him with first a question, then understanding, finally acceptance in his eyes. He waited by the river until Donovan reached them but he didn't make the policeman explain his presence. 'All right, officer, I'm coming now. We're finished here.'

David looked between the two men in sharp-eyed bewilderment. 'What the hell's going on? Donovan?'

Payne turned to him slowly, like a man finding his coat-tails tugged by a child. 'I'm afraid that's as much as we can do. I expect it'll be enough.' He managed a wan smile. 'Though you may find an unexpectedly heavy demand.'

'What are you *talking* about?'

'I'm sorry, David, I have to go. Would you take the car back to my house and put the keys through the letter-box before you leave?'

'No, sorry,' Donovan said quickly, 'I need you at the station too. Inspector Graham'll explain. I'll have someone take your car home, Mr Payne.'

Payne accepted that too with a gracious shrug. In fact the situation was now out of his hands and he had no say in what happened next. But it was Donovan's experience that the higher standing a man enjoyed in society, the harder he found it to accept that. The genuine criminal classes, who really did on occasion say, 'It's a fair cop, guv,' were much easier to arrest.

Donovan had two cars at the scene. He sent David back in one, travelled with Payne in the other. It would seem natural enough to David that the detective sergeant would ride with the suspect rather than the witness. Actually it was a way to avoid questions he didn't want to answer.

Frank Shapiro's face was tight with anger and his eyes were hollow with shock. 'I don't believe this,' he said, more than once. 'It's not possible, I don't believe it.'

'It is possible,' said Liz carefully, speaking as clearly as if to a child, 'but that's all it is. If I've got this wrong, Frank, nobody'll be happier than me.'

'I don't understand,' he said, also not for the first time. 'How can you think David's capable of such a thing? Of killing someone, for God's sake – a man died in one of those fires. Whatever makes you think my son is capable of that? He's not an easy boy, God knows, he always had more – resolve – than he knew what to do with, but still, Liz, murder?'

Before she could answer Donovan put his head round the door to say they'd arrived. 'Who do you want to interview first?'

Liz said, 'David,' and Shapiro said, 'Yes, all right, we can dispose of this nonsense in five minutes and get on with something serious.'

She looked at him with compassion but no yielding. 'Frank, I'm sorry to be blunt but you have no part in this. It's my case, David's my suspect, and I don't want you there when I question him. You've been kept informed as a matter of professional courtesy, but that's it: from here on your son will be treated the same as any other interviewee. I'll tell David his rights before we start: if he wants a solicitor present that's something you can do for him. But he's too old to need or even want his father present during questioning.'

She was right, but there was no mistaking the hurt she caused him. He dropped his eyes quickly and she heard him take a deep breath. Then he reached for the phone.

'I'll call my solicitor. At least wait till he gets here.'

But David didn't want a solicitor present, perhaps least of all his father's solicitor, so she couldn't even grant him that. She began the interview at two fifteen, with five hours in hand before Castle Mall opened. A fact of no significance if David Shapiro were the man she sought but of pressing urgency if he were not.

For ten minutes Shapiro sat alone in his office, his chin sunk on his chest and his eyes veiled as if he were dozing. But behind the mask of stillness his mind was racing. He was trying to remember how they ever got here: from the proudest night of his life, when he'd held up the red and squawling thing fresh from its mother's belly, to sitting in a silent room waiting to learn if that same child had taken its rejection of everything he stood for so far as to repeatedly risk and finally take a human life.

He ached for the certainty in his own heart that it wasn't possible, that Liz had made a silly mistake and would be back any moment to apologize for it. But he couldn't be that sure. It wasn't that he didn't know his son any more; he'd never known him, never understood him, never known what he was capable of.

After ten minutes he suddenly lurched to his feet, rammed his fists into his pockets and stalked downstairs.

Taylor looked up at his unheralded arrival with a guilty start Shapiro didn't understand until he saw what the Superintendent was doing. He was looking at the photographs of his children on his desk.

'Wait till we know there's something to sympathize about before you say There But For the Grace of God,' he grunted.

Taylor pushed the picture-frames away quickly. 'Yes, of course.'

'Inspector Graham's talking to him,' said Shapiro. 'Meanwhile Payne's twiddling his thumbs in the other interview room. Is there any objection to me questioning him?'

Taylor had to think about that, but in fact there wasn't. There was no longer a shadow hanging over Shapiro's conduct of the case. He jailed the wrong man, but that was something that could happen to any of them and particularly to anyone who didn't have all the evidence. 'If you're sure you want to. I'd understand if you were too upset by . . . this other business . . . to handle it.'

'Of course I'm upset,' snapped Shapiro. 'But it's David's problem, there's nothing I can do about it. But BMT was my case: I may not have distinguished myself over it, but I'd rather wrap it up myself than have someone else do it.'

'Yes, all right,' agreed Taylor. 'But be careful, Frank. Complaints'll be going over the thing with a fine-tooth comb: I don't want them to find any more irregularities. Question Payne by all means, take a statement if you can. But by the book, all right? I know how you must feel about him, but keep a lid on it. I don't want anything else to go wrong.'

As Shapiro headed for the door Taylor called after him, 'Get Donovan to give you a hand.'

Shapiro turned slowly and his eyes were molten. 'I thought he was helping Inspector Graham.'

'Not at the moment. Have him sit in with you: it might be hard to remember sometimes but he is a sergeant; if there are any queries afterwards he'll be a useful witness.'

'Witness.' Shapiro pondered. 'You mean, he'll be able to corroborate my account of the suspect suddenly head-butting the recording equipment.'

Superintendent Taylor was not gifted with a great sense of humour. Many of Shapiro's little witticisms passed him by. But he smiled at that one. Perhaps he thought it safest.

Shapiro sighed. 'All right.' He turned towards the interview rooms, and Donovan was at his heel when he got there.

4

Keaton Payne the naturalist and Frank Shapiro the detective had never met. Shapiro knew Payne's face from the television and newspapers. Payne knew Shapiro's from his bad dreams.

'I knew eight years ago that it was you I had to worry about.' The smile was rueful but without bitterness or any sense of enmity. Payne seemed to think this could be done as politely as one general accepting another's sword. 'I had you in mind when I was planning it. There wasn't much time, I had to strike while indignation was running high. Going on television was a bad move for BMT, there was quite a backlash and while it lasted I could count on widespread public sympathy. But I had to be careful. I knew better than to expect sympathy from you.'

'I'll take that as a compliment, shall I?' said Shapiro, expressionless.

'Oh do,' said Payne, 'it's most sincerely meant.'

'To what extent were the darts players involved?'

Payne shook the leonine head. 'Merely as a diversion. I knew you'd be expecting a reaction to the broadcast and have the laboratory under surveillance. I needed fifteen minutes to get in, free the animals, torch the place and get out. But whoever drew your fire had to be able to stand up to questioning. It didn't matter what you suspected as long as you could prove nothing against them.

'When I found a darts team with a forthcoming fixture in Castlemere I had them bring it forward. They told the

180

pub team they couldn't make the agreed date, offered to buy the drinks if it could be done at short notice. The Castlemere team were all local men, a few phone calls was all it took.'

'Did the darts players know what you intended?'

'No,' Payne said firmly. 'They thought that our sole purpose in entering the laboratory was to free the animals. Only my squad knew I meant to burn the place.'

'Your squad?' murmured Shapiro.

Payne gave a lofty smile. 'Be your age, Chief Inspector. I'll tell you what happened but I won't give you names. You've got me: don't be greedy.'

'So the darts team hared off in their van with the police car in pursuit, and you broke into the laboratory, removed the animals and set incendiaries. Did you know there was a security guard?'

'Of course,' Payne said readily. 'Research was my speciality. There were usually two men on duty but one of them had 'flu and with the police about he wasn't replaced. That left one man in the porter's lodge inside the main entrance.'

'How did you know he'd be in the office, not walking the corridors?'

'It didn't matter where he was: we rang the front-door bell and he let us in. I had on a dark coat and a chequered cap, he thought I was one of your men. By the time he realized his mistake it was too late. Two of our lads stayed with him while we got the job done. When we were ready to leave we shut him in an outbuilding. He'd have been all right if he'd stayed there.'

'He was paid to protect the premises. He broke out of the shed and returned to his office to raise the alarm. But you'd cut the phone line, hadn't you? So he went to see about the animals. He knew you'd opened the cages, he wasn't sure they'd find their way outside.'

Payne nodded sombrely. 'I read that in the paper. I felt badly about it. But I told him they were safe. He should have known we wouldn't leave them to burn.'

Shapiro said levelly, 'Well, as long as you felt badly about it.'

If he'd been caught at the time of the raid, Red Kenny the scourge of the vivisectors would have been mentally prepared for anything the police might throw at him, up to and including the furniture. But eight years of highly public success had changed his expectations. He was used to being listened to with respect and admiration, had come to take it as his right. He had not so much fallen as dived headlong with a flourish into the pitfall specially designed for television celebrities, that of believing in his own myth. He'd heard so often what a splendid fellow he was that he thought it must be so. He resented being spoken to in a manner suggesting that in some quarters these truths were somewhat less than self-evident.

He frowned. 'I know you can't approve of what I did, Chief Inspector, but try to remember why we were there. It wasn't for the good of our health. There was no money in it. We were there because BioMedical Technology routinely performed painful, distressing and lethal experiments on animals, and they did it for profit. Not in pursuit of a cure for cancer, but so that women who were born white might look a little browner when brown is in fashion, and women who were born brown might straighten their hair when it isn't.

'Do you know what an LD50 test is? You take a statistically significant sample of animals and subject them to increasing levels of a substance until fifty per cent of them are alive and fifty per cent dead. The amount of scientifically useful information that gives you wouldn't displace a single angel from the proverbial pin-head. It's useful to know what overdose of a substance is potentially fatal, but you know that when you've got your first corpse. There is no value in knowing how much of a substance will kill half your mice: all of them after the first one die for nothing. OK, they're only mice. But they have the same capacity to feel pain that we have, and their lives are all they've got. They shouldn't be used and thrown away for nothing. It's immoral.'

'So is killing people.'

'I never intended to hurt anyone except financially,' Payne said frostily. 'I'm sorry about the security guard, but I'm not responsible for either his asthma or the fact that he returned to a burning building.'

'What about Trevor Foot? Do you feel any responsibility for what happened to him?'

Payne met his gaze squarely. 'No. Do you?'

'Since you ask,' said Shapiro, his lip curling, 'yes. I should never have believed a little toe-rag like that was behind something this slick. It had to be someone like you. If I'd kept looking I'd have found you.'

That was more the sort of comment a television scientist expected. 'Can I take *that* as a compliment?'

'Actually,' said Shapiro, 'no. Go on with the story.'

Payne gave a cool shrug. 'There's nothing more to tell. That was BEAST's last action. I finished my research, left Cambridge, and what I've done since is a matter of record. I don't regret BEAST but I suppose I grew beyond it. I make my voice heard in other ways now, without risking my safety and my freedom.'

Suddenly he laughed. 'Which is why, of course, I found myself playing the reluctant host to your son. You could have knocked me down with a feather when he introduced himself. The magazine said they'd be sending a photographer but they didn't say who. When I realized who he was I couldn't think what to do. I'm afraid I rather panicked. I made up some feeble excuse and sent him away.'

'He thought you didn't want a Jew in your house.'

Payne's eyes widened. 'What kind of man does he take me for?' He said it without any trace of irony. 'I didn't know how close you'd got to BEAST before, didn't want

183

to remind you I was still about. At that point, of course, I didn't know that you two hardly speak.'

Shapiro's jaw hardened but he didn't comment. 'Why did you change your mind?'

'I realized I was behaving as if I had something to hide. It was a coincidence, nothing more – if you had finally tracked me down you wouldn't have sent your son. Then when it was in the paper that the Foot case was being reopened I thought I could learn something useful from him, so I called him back.

'I have to say, young David was a bit of a disappointment. He wouldn't talk about you however much I prompted. Apart from telling me how to stand and when to blink, the only time he opened up was when he talked about his ambitions. He'll do well, you know. If you want something as much as he wants that, you don't let anything stand in your way.'

'Can we leave my son's ambitions out of this?' Shapiro asked coldly. 'I'd like to hear why you let Trevor Foot go to prison for what you did.'

'Isn't it obvious? I didn't want to go myself.'

Shapiro shook his head in disbelief. But he shouldn't have been surprised: he'd dealt with professional criminals and he'd dealt with fanatics, and for ruthlessness fanatics had the edge every time. 'It really is that simple? You'd sacrifice anyone to get what you want?'

'No, not anyone. But you said it yourself: Foot's a toerag. Lazy, dishonest, a bore and a bigot. What would he have done with his freedom? He'd still be a painter and decorator, unless he'd got the sack by now. He'd still be joining every lunatic fringe group in town. And he'd still be trooping in to your front desk at intervals to claim the Crime of the Month. He's been a public nuisance all his life: the only positive thing he ever did was to keep me out of prison.'

Such arrogance would have been staggering in any circumstances. What made it devastating was the man's clear belief that it was a fair trade: eight years of an innocent boring man's time for eight years of an important guilty one's. He thought that because he was a cleverer man than Foot, and had been acting in a cause and had gone on to become a public figure who appeared on television and opened church fêtes, his freedom weighed more on the cosmic scale than Foot's. Even now he failed to appreciate the enormity of what he'd done.

'Hang on,' said Shapiro, suddenly aware that there was an implication here that he was missing. That description was too accurate to have been gleaned from newspaper reports. 'Are you telling me you *knew* Trevor Foot?'

'Oh yes,' said Payne. He grinned boyishly. 'Better than he knew us. Don't misunderstand, Chief Inspector, he was never a member of BEAST. But it wasn't for want of trying. A few of us lived around here so some of our activities were in this area; of course, you're aware of that. It seemed to make us fair game. He kept trying to contact us: he'd dog anyone who spoke up for animal rights or against blood sports, anything like that. In the end he was reduced to spying on vegetarians.

'We strung him along. For light relief, you know? Look, we were playing a game that could have finished all our careers and put half of us in prison. We needed to let off steam sometimes. Foot was a standing joke. When we'd nothing better to do we'd slip him messages – he worked around the town, it was easy to leave a note in his pocket while his coat hung on a fencepost or put it on the front seat of his van – inviting him to the next meeting. It was always somewhere inaccessible and whenever possible on a wet night. We warned him that if the authorities got wind of us we'd vanish into the night so he should never wait more than a couple of hours.'

He chuckled at Shapiro's expression. 'I know what you're thinking: we should have had more important things to do than torment the village idiot. But he brought it on himself. We were all so exasperated it was a choice between that and breaking his legs.'

'Broken legs wouldn't have taken eight years to mend.'

But Shapiro's mind was on something else. He was thinking, in some despair: everything Foot said was true. The girl. The trip to London. Even the messages he received. I assumed he'd made it up. There was no proof he was lying, I just assumed it – because of who he was, because I knew him and the things he got involved with.

I could have got to the bottom of it if I'd kept looking – not got to this man, no, there were too many people ready to shield him, but the evidence was there that Foot wasn't involved. If I'd looked I'd have found it. If I hadn't fallen into the trap I warn every new DC against: presuming we know more about a case than the facts warrant. I didn't frame Trevor Foot but I might as well have done. I cocked up, and he went to prison because of it.

'Doesn't it worry you?' he asked. 'That for being a pain in the neck you let a man rot for eight years? Seeing animals behind bars incensed you enough to risk your own liberty: doesn't it trouble you that you locked an innocent man away?'

'I didn't send him to prison,' Payne said indignantly. 'I didn't accuse him, convict him or sentence him. I used him, yes; in fact, we both did. I used him to protect me from a law that values property above humanity. You used him to tidy up your crime figures. That may damage my chances of an Albert Schweitzer Award, but it doesn't leave you smelling of roses either.'

'You're telling me something I don't know already?' snapped Shapiro. 'I know what a mess I made of this, not only by locking him up but by leaving you free. Well, I can do something about the latter, but all I can do about the former is regret it. I don't suppose that'll be much consolation to Trevor Foot. But stupid as I was, I bore him no malice. If I had to admit that I ruined his life out of spite, I think I'd die of shame.'

He stood up. 'Don't tell me, I know how much my opinion's worth to you. Well now, could you use a cup of tea? Afterwards we'll get it all down as a statement.'

186

He left the interview room and Donovan followed him out. Because he was angry with himself Shapiro looked for someone to take it out on. 'You were a lot of use in there. I thought you'd died and it was sheer force of habit keeping you leaning against the wall. There's only the introduction on the tape to show you were in the room.'

Donovan shrugged. 'You didn't seem to need any help.'

'Appearances can be deceptive,' the Chief Inspector muttered grimly, heading down the corridor.

5

In a world which equates power with sound – the roar of a jet engine, the tumult of raised voices, the quake of marching feet – it's easy to forget the strength there may be in silence. David Shapiro discovered that strength early in life and learned to use it to maximum effect. With it he reduced a good, kind, intelligent man to impotent despair.

Liz Graham was also good, intelligent and reasonably kind, but she had two massive advantages over Shapiro in handling his son. She was not a man, and she was not his parent. Nature tells females how to deal with unruly young things, because if it didn't few of them would grow to be old things. Also, to her David was just another suspect. She was sorry for Shapiro, but not enough to give his son an easy ride.

She knew she could breach his defences with not much more than time, patience and a smattering of good humour. But there was no time. It was imperative to establish whether they were still looking for an arsonist or not. David's refusal to communicate posed a real threat: people could die because of it. In these precise circumstances he was more dangerous innocent than guilty.

Yet with disaster snapping at her heels Liz could only chip away at the stone and hope to find the truth waiting inside like a sculpture. She sighed and started again.

'So you left London about six on Saturday morning in order to be at Payne's house for nine o'clock. Yes?'

'Yes,' said David Shapiro leadenly.

'But your last job was on the Thursday, and you can't think of anyone who could put you in the city after the fire at the corner shop on the Friday night.'

'No.'

'Friends, neighbours, clients? Nobody phoned you at home?'

'No.'

'At any event you were in Castlemere on Monday night when the warehouse burned down, and on Tuesday night when the timberyard was torched just metres from where you were sleeping.'

'Yes.'

'But you deny causing any of these fires.'

'Yes.'

'Can you see how I might have a problem believing that?'

He didn't bother to answer that, even to shrug.

'You seem to be interested in fire.'

'Most photographers will follow a fire engine.'

'Most news photographers,' Liz said pointedly. 'But you're not a news photographer, are you? But you want to be. When you have the portfolio.' No answer. 'You got some good shots at the timberyard.'

He didn't rise to the bait, only gave her a cynic smile and said, 'Thank you.'

She changed tack. 'Were you going to the opening of the Castle Mall this evening?'

His eyes were disdainful. 'Not my scene, Inspector.'

'The *Courier* will want some pictures.'

'Of course they will. They've got advertisers to keep happy. That's why they'll have their own man there.' It was the longest reply he'd given since they began.

'So you're not interested.'

He grinned with sudden vivid ferocity. 'Only if it catches fire.'

She kept her gaze level. 'Have you some reason to think it might?'

189

For the first time since he realized he was here to talk about himself not Payne he seemed shaken. 'Are you kidding?'

Liz shook her head. 'Not even slightly. David, I'm terrified that several thousand people are going to cram in there, to see the bands and the fireworks and the celebrities, and maybe even look at the shops, and while their kids are running about the concourse and their old mums are tripping people up with their walking-sticks somebody's going to stage an entertainment of his own. I've no proof. All I've got's a gut feeling. But I know – in here I know' – she tapped between her breasts – 'that that's the next target.

'David, if it's you, please, please say so. It can't do you any harm now. You're not leaving here until I know one way or the other, so if it is you that started these fires there's no chance of you burning the Mall. Help me now and I'll help you as best I can. And if it isn't you, convince me. Then I can stop wasting my time and concentrate on protecting those people. Three hours from now the place will be packed. If it burns down because you put the pleasure of giving me a hard time over the safety of all those people, the consequences will be as much your fault as if you set the fire.'

She thought from his face that she'd got to him. But all he said was, 'Not legally.'

'Stuff legally!' she spat, her patience snapping. 'I'm talking about people's lives! About people burning to death. Trapped in a panicking crowd and burning to death.'

Whatever his shortcomings, David Shapiro was not an unfeeling man. The image hit him in the belly like a fist: Liz saw the shockwaves flicker through his eyes. There was a movement there as of something crumbling; then all at once he was naked before her, a scared twenty-three-year-old out of his depth, not waving but drowning. Without the armour of his brittle anger to defend him he was vulnerable: a young man lacking the experience to

190

deal with the situation in which he found himself, accused of monstrous things and not knowing how to refute them.

He understood what she was saying: that standing on his right to silence could cost lives. He understood what that meant: heaving bodies jamming the exits, screams choking as the air grew too hot to breathe, those in front crushed into an impenetrable barrier confining those behind till they burned. For a second he tasted the hot smoke and the barbecue smell. The little colour he had drained away. His eyes closed.

'I don't know what you want me to say.' His voice was thin. 'I've told you, it wasn't me. I didn't do these things. Yes, I could have done – except the first, I was still in London – but I didn't. You want me to prove it? I can't. How many people could? Maybe you – you have colleagues, I expect you have a family, you're in the town where you live, maybe you could produce witnesses to vouch for your whereabouts at all the material times. But I live alone, and for the most part I work alone, and there are millions of people in London who wouldn't remember me two minutes after I left them.

'I have a flat in an old house, right? My nearest neighbour is a deaf old lady who puts notes through my door when she needs a box of matches or a bottle of milk. She doesn't knock on the door because she thinks I'm always out. I'm not, I'm there half the day, I have my dark-room there, but the woman on the other side of my wall thinks I'm out. There are two other flats in the house but one of them's empty and the other changes from week to week. I don't know the name of the man there now, and anyway he'll probably have gone when I get back. My local shop's a supermarket, and I don't drink enough to be a regular in the pub.

'Do you understand? If I die in my bed one night nobody'll miss me. I'll lie there decomposing till the old lady writes a note to the council complaining about the smell.

'What more can I say? I've told you the truth. You

191

don't believe me. What do you want me to do about that? If I change my story and confess, you won't believe it after tonight, and by then you'll have a razed building and a lot of dead and injured people. So what do you want from me? I should cross my heart and hope to die? You've got it. Any oath you want me to take, I'll take it. But I can't make you believe me.'

She might have believed him. She could have accepted that he couldn't prove his alibi for the first fire, and that while he was in town for the later two so were fifty thousand other people. She could have accepted professional interest as an explanation for his presence at the scenes of two crimes. But she hit real difficulties when she tried to get round what Mary McKenna told her about the fire at Castle High.

She took a deep breath to steady her jangling nerves, caught and held his eyes. She said quietly, 'Tell me that what you did in your last term at school here was a one-off. That it was a stupid teenage prank. That you only did it to see if you could, and the results scared the wits out of you so you never tried it again. Tell me that and I just might believe you.'

His eyes, which were unexpectedly blue, the only colour in the chiaroscuro frame of his pale face and dark hair, were both wild and bewildered. His voice wavered between exasperation and a plaint. 'What prank? I don't know what you're talking about. I don't know what you want.'

It was like playing a fish: watching him thrash, drawing him closer, giving him enough line that it didn't break, not giving him so much that he could dart away and hide in the tangled weeds of invention. Liz was close to the truth now: she could feel it, this was where it lurked, if she could keep him here she would have it.

'The fire in the chemistry lab,' she said. 'I know about it, I've talked to Ms McKenna.'

'And she said that was *me*?' His voice cracked.

'David, she knew! OK, she couldn't prove it, but she knew it was you. Your dad knew it was you. That's what's been wrong between you, isn't it? – that he knew what you'd done, and he didn't shop you, but he's never forgiven you for putting him in that position. That's the truth of the matter, isn't it?'

'No, God damn it, it's not!' He came halfway to his feet, leaning over the table, his white face shouting into hers. Scobie, who was sitting in on the interview, made a move towards him but Liz flicked her hand at him, waving him back almost contemptuously. David Shapiro wasn't going to hit her, and if he tried she was more than his match. He frightened her no more than a child in a tantrum. 'You've got it all wrong. That wasn't me—'

Liz pushed him away from her firmly enough that he landed with a thump back in his chair. 'This is absurd. If you're going to deny things that half the town knows you did, how can I believe a word you say?' She stood up abruptly. 'Scobie, get the Chief. Let's at least get this bit of nonsense sorted out. If we could stop arguing over the patently true, maybe we could make a bit of progress on something that matters. Though I have to tell you, David,' she added as Scobie left the room, 'I'm about as convinced as I need to be that while I keep you here the Mall is safe.'

Scobie hadn't far to go to find Chief Inspector Shapiro: they all but collided as he left the room. 'Inspector Graham would like your assistance, sir.'

'About time too.' Shapiro gave the door a perfunctory rap and walked in.

Liz hadn't expected to have to comb the building but she was nettled that he'd been waiting outside the door. She gave him a tight little smile. 'Frank, we could use a bit of help here. I want to talk about the incident at the school in his last term there but David seems to have forgotten about it.'

Shapiro looked at his inspector. He looked at his son.

193

He even looked at Scobie, which people tended not to do unless they were all out of options. He pushed his fists deep into his pockets. 'What incident?'

Liz felt her eyes rounding as her gaze turned into a stare. She waited, a little breathlessly, for him to explain but he didn't. She thought, My God, Donovan's right! He's covered it up, and even now he's going to try and bluff it out.

They were all watching her with interest, waiting to see what she'd do now. When the time came that somebody had to say something she blinked her smarting eyes and said, with rigid self-control, 'The fire. In the chemistry lab. That Ms McKenna told you was probably David's handiwork.'

Shapiro met her gaze without flinching. 'Ms McKenna never told me any such thing.'

'Well, she says she did.'

'If that's what she says, she's lying.'

'Why on earth would she?'

'I can't imagine.'

It was a stand-off. There was no room left for it to be a misunderstanding: somebody was lying to her, and it was either Mary McKenna who seemed to have no possible reason or Frank Shapiro who had a reason but on whose honesty she would have staked her pension. She winced at that. Before this week she'd have staked her life.

David started to say, 'You don't understand—' But nobody present was interested in his opinion for the moment. His father snapped, 'Shut up, David,' without taking his eyes off Liz, and Liz said coldly, also without looking at him, 'You had your chance to talk, now leave it to the grown-ups.'

She'd faced down a lot of hard, vicious men in her time. Most were criminals, some were just nasty bastards, a few were colleagues. She'd dealt with them all, and if she didn't exactly enjoy a confrontation the way men often did experience had taught her two things: that the other

194

guy would blink first, and that she wouldn't lose any sleep afterwards.

Going eyeball to eyeball with a man she cared about was something different. She didn't want to do it, not in front of his son and one of their constables. If there'd been a way out she'd have taken it. But the issue was just too damned important; and her self-respect was important too. She hadn't created this situation, Shapiro had. Any fallout would be his responsibility.

She said, 'Shall I send for the file? Or do you remember now that there was a fire at Castle High about six years ago and you were the investigating officer?'

'I remember the fire,' said Shapiro. 'But I didn't investigate it. I wasn't even in the country at the time. Neither was David.'

She blinked then. '*What?*'

'That was the year we went to Israel. The last family holiday we had. That photo on my desk? That was taken then. I know it was that fortnight because it wasn't a resounding success, and when we got back I said I wasn't going on any more holidays, I'd have had more fun poking through the ashes at Castle High. And David said he felt the same way.'

Liz was confused. 'If you didn't head the investigation, who did? Ms McKenna said—' Then she remembered exactly what Ms McKenna had said and her jaw fell. Her voice was a shocked whisper. 'Jesus, Frank, I think I've been rather stupid. She said, my chief. Not my chief inspector – my chief.'

'If memory serves me right,' said Shapiro carefully, 'and I think it does though we'd better check the file, Mr Taylor handled that one personally.'

'That's what I was trying to tell you,' said David, finally getting a word in edgeways. 'It was an open secret in school, who was supposed to have torched the lab. Robin Taylor. The word was he only got away with it because of who his father was.

195

'I denied it, of course,' he added, his tone icy, his eyes smoking. 'I said it didn't work like that, being a copper's son. I said the law of England may presume innocence until it proves guilt but coppers presume their kids are crap unless they can prove otherwise. I said any copper who thought his kid had done that not only wouldn't cover up for him, he'd want his own name on the charge sheet.'

6

As soon as Shapiro came into his office Superintendent Taylor knew something had happened. There was a stillness about him, even as he moved, and no expression on the broad face, but his eyes were sombre and perceptive. Until he'd heard what Taylor had to say he wanted to keep his feelings to himself. But his eyes betrayed him. When the Superintendent saw compassion there he knew what it was that Shapiro had found out.

But he was a cautious man, and the possibility that he was wrong made him circumspect. He matched Shapiro cool for cool, and within the natural boundary of his whiskers guarded his expression as carefully. He said evenly, 'What can I do for you, Frank?'

It is difficult to condense important issues into a few sentences. Sometimes the only choice is between saying everything and saying almost nothing. With time more pressing than ever, a full unburdening of souls would have to wait. 'Where's Robin?'

It was in fact a superbly concise and effective summary that told Taylor all he needed to know. There was only one reason for Shapiro to have asked that now. Despite all Taylor's efforts to frustrate him he had somehow stumbled on to the truth. No, that was unfair: a detective didn't put together a catalogue of successes like Shapiro's by floundering around until good fortune tripped him up. He said, 'At home.'

'Are you sure?'

'Quite sure. My brother's with him.'

Shapiro sat down, subsiding into the chair like an airship settling. Compared with the trim figure opposite, the perfection of his grooming testament to a rigorous self-discipline, the Detective Chief Inspector looked old and weary and sad. 'Do you want to tell me about it or shall I get someone down from HQ?'

Taylor gave a small pained smile. 'Of course I'll tell you about it, Frank. You're a fundamental part of it.'

Shapiro frowned. 'I don't understand.'

'You will.'

Liz took Donovan and Scobie to Superintendent Taylor's house on Cambridge Road. She didn't know how much trouble she was likely to have with his son the pyromaniac. Quite possibly none: there are compulsive personalities who are perfectly decent people outside the ambit of their particular obsession. If Robin Taylor was one it would be an easy arrest and he'd probably make a full admission as soon as he was asked. The whys and wherefores could wait, but Liz wanted confirmation that the crowds attending Castle Mall would be safe. When she had that she would relax for the first time in a week.

With twenty-four hours to go to the wedding the household was in chaos. A group of men – too many of them, to Liz's eye, with too little idea of what they were doing – were trying to erect a striped marquee on the lawn. The door was answered by the bride-to-be, fetchingly attired in jeans and a veil, who directed her to the kitchen and reminded her that a small vegetarian selection was required as well.

Liz tried not to smile. 'I'm not here to do the buffet.' She introduced herself. 'It's Robin I want to see.'

Alison Taylor may not have known that her twin brother was pursuing an active career as an arsonist but she knew there was a problem. Instead of shouting for him or telling Liz where to look she said quietly, 'I'll fetch my mother.'

Liz waited in the hall, Scobie on the doorstep, and Donovan prowled off round the side of the house. He didn't say anything and Liz didn't ask but he was covering the rear exit. The back lane, where the skip was parked in which Ted Burton dumped his empty oil can, ran along the foot of the gardens.

There were a handful of social functions each year when police spouses were rolled out, at which Mrs Taylor was a gracious hostess and to which Liz had to drag Brian, complaining, in a dinner-jacket that did nothing for him. So they knew one another at least casually, and it seemed significant to Liz that Mrs Taylor, coming down the stairs with an armful of silk flowers, quietly addressed her not by name but by her title.

'I believe Robin is in the garden, Inspector. My brother-in-law is with him.'

Nor was that the non sequitur it sounded. The Taylors knew what they were dealing with: it was second nature to them always to know where their son was and who was watching him. To an extent that made them accomplices. It would be difficult to plead ignorance of his activities when such measures had been deemed a necessary part of family life. That, plus the fact that she was dealing with the personal affairs of her superintendent, made Liz choose her words carefully. 'Is that Major Taylor's . . . role?'

June Taylor was a woman of fifty, short enough and broad enough that even those who loved her could find no other description than 'dumpy'. She presented the same outline as Queen Victoria at the same age, and wore her greying hair in a not dissimilar style. There was also something slightly regal about her manner. She struck Liz as a kind woman but not necessarily a warm one.

There was little warmth in either her voice with its soft Scottish accent or her eyes when she said, 'Ian is my husband's brother, that's his role. He's here for his niece's wedding. But yes, he helps supervise our son. This is a family occasion, and Robin is part of our family. We

199

wanted him here. Ian's help made it possible.'

'Where does Robin live, Mrs Taylor?'

'In Switzerland. He tells people he works for the World Health Organization, but of course that isn't true. It's called a clinic but actually it's a residential home where they undertake to keep him out of trouble. Where, if they fail, at least he's off my husband's manor.' She spoke with such refinement that it didn't sound like slang, more as if the Superintendent were the laird of some great estate.

'Until this time?'

Mrs Taylor smiled, still without warmth, and ended the interview as smoothly as a professional. 'I don't think I wish to say anything more at this point, Inspector.' Stately as royal progress she turned towards the door. 'Come along and we'll find Robin.'

'You mustn't think,' said Superintendent Taylor, 'that we sent Robin abroad to get rid of him. The Amin Clinic has an international reputation in the treatment of sociopathic illness. Once we realized we had a major problem we had three priorities: to get help for the boy, to ensure that he couldn't hurt anyone and to protect the family. Too many families break up over mental illness. We didn't want that. We had a daughter to raise as well as a son: if we'd tried to keep Robin at home our whole lives would've had to revolve around him, and that wouldn't have been fair to Alison. Any of us, in fact. We all had lives to lead. We needed to care for Robin without sacrificing ourselves.'

'When did you realize it was more than a phase he was going through?' Shapiro's voice was hypnotically quiet. His skill as an investigator lay only partly in his ability to ram home the pointed question with anatomical accuracy. He got as many results this way: gently, persistently probing, spinning a thread of sympathy between himself and his suspects. As the interview developed, many of them came to see it as a lifeline. He didn't make rash promises, but people whose lives had been turned upside-down by violence – even if it was their own – drew comfort from the solidity of his presence. They felt he was someone they could trust, and told him the truth because lying would be like lying to Father Christmas.

Of course, the Father Confessor approach didn't work with everyone. He could, at need, do a fair impression of the Spanish Inquisition as well.

Superintendent Taylor sighed. 'That episode at the school. It wasn't the first but it was the first serious one, the first where people could have got hurt. I couldn't believe he'd done that: deliberately started a fire in a building occupied by twelve hundred children.

'You were away that week, and DI Clarke was at the county court: I was about the only senior officer in the station so I went myself. Lucky I did; or perhaps not. If I hadn't been able to protect him, perhaps it wouldn't have gone this far.'

'We all try to protect our children, James,' Shapiro said quietly.

'Oh, sure. But some of us try too hard.' He paused to organize his thoughts. 'I was knocked sideways by Ms McKenna's suggestion. There was no proof, she said so herself; my first instinct was to tell her either to produce some evidence or keep her insinuations to herself. But when I thought about it, when I discussed it with June, we knew it was true.

'So I looked for some help. There were obvious advantages in sending him abroad – I didn't want it to become public knowledge in Castlemere, there would be times it would get in the way of my job – all the same, I wouldn't have sent him unless I'd thought they could help him. It was for six months initially. Then twelve. Then they said they couldn't guarantee his behaviour without continuing supervision. In effect they were saying that my son needed to be locked up for the foreseeable future if he wasn't to be a public menace. We talked about it and decided, for the same reasons that we sent him there, that he should stay.'

Shapiro said, 'It must have been a difficult decision. It sounds like it was the right one.'

'Oh, it was.' Taylor cast him a look that spoke of more to come. 'It was the best we could do, the best life we could give Robin without endangering anyone else's, and it worked for six years. We visit him three or four times a year, write every week, send him photographs. We didn't abandon him, Frank. We didn't forget him. We didn't even stop loving him. And he seemed happy there. Settled. We thought the worst was over.

'When we started planning Alison's wedding, it seemed awful to exclude her twin brother. We asked the clinic: they said Robin had been better this last year, if we wanted to take him home for a couple of weeks as long as we kept an eye on him there shouldn't be any problem. I knew I couldn't be with him constantly, and June would have too much to do with the wedding, so I asked Ian if he'd baby-sit.'

'So what went wrong?'

Taylor gave a little despairing laugh. 'Everything. Beginning with fog at Heathrow so that his flight was diverted to Stansted. Ian was picking him up on his way over – he's based in Surrey – and by the time he got to Stansted the boy had disappeared. This was last Friday week. He turned up with the milk on Saturday morning, apologized for worrying us, said he'd got a lift with some people he met on the plane and ended up going to a party with them. Then when I went into the office my up-date included the fire at the corner shop.

'I'd no reason to suppose it was Robin. At that point it could have been an accident, an electrical fault, anything – nobody even mentioned arson till later. So I can't say I was suspicious. It just made me extra-careful for a few days.'

'Until about Monday?'

202

Taylor gave a helpless shrug. 'We thought he was asleep. I checked before I went to bed and he was there then. I locked up, set the alarm; I thought he was safe. And he was back in his room next morning, and the alarm was still working. But he must have figured out how to switch it off. I know that now. I know it was him burned the warehouse. But then I didn't think it could be. I want you to believe that.'

Shapiro nodded gravely. 'All right.'

'Tuesday night he went out again. Same thing: he switched off the alarm, let himself out and disappeared. He came back about six in the morning, the smell of smoke on his clothes and his hands reeking of petrol. I know because I was waiting for him. Ian had looked in on him quarter of an hour before – he's a soldier, he's used to an early start – and woke me when he found he was missing.

'But it was not my brother's responsibility,' he added firmly. 'The arrangement was, Ian would supervise him during the day when I couldn't be there, and I'd spell him at night when I could. What happened is my fault: not Ian's, not Robin's.

'Well, now I knew what the situation was. Robin wasn't cured, he's still a very dangerous young man. He had no access to the cars, mine and June's, so he syphoned petrol out of the lawn-mower into an oil can he found in the lane. How can you anticipate something like that?

'But once I knew what we had to do to keep him safe, we could do it. It was hard work, it meant precious little sleep for any of us, but it was possible. I could guarantee there'd be no more incidents. A few more days and Alison would be wed, and we could take him back to the clinic – I wouldn't risk him travelling alone again – and nobody any the wiser. If he went back early, before the wedding, people would wonder why. I was afraid someone would remember about the school and put two and two together. I decided to sit it out.'

'A man died, James,' Shapiro reminded him softly. 'At the timberyard. A dosser, Robin probably never knew he was there. But the fire killed him. You had no right covering for him after that.'

Taylor's eyes blazed in a furious agony, the most emotion Shapiro had ever seen there. 'Do you think I don't know that? Do you think I can justify what I did? Even when I was doing it I didn't think it was right. I'm a policeman, for God's sake, I know the difference between right and wrong. But it goes deeper than that. He's my child: all the rules and regulations in the world don't alter the fact that when your children need your help you do what you can for them.'

'Even if it means hounding other people's?' Shapiro thought he'd kept the anger out of his voice but Taylor was aware of it.

'That wasn't my idea, Frank. Liz Graham thought it could be David. What was I to say? That I knew it couldn't be your son who was burning the town down because it was mine? I let her get on with it. I knew she couldn't prove anything. I knew there wouldn't be any more fires. It was a waste of her time, and a bit unpleasant for David, but that was all. No harm could come of it. All I needed was forty-eight hours and Robin would be safely back in Switzerland.'

'No harm?' echoed Shapiro breathlessly. Again it was a choice between saying nearly nothing and too much. He gave a little shake of his head. 'James, I've been worried sick.'

'Yes. I'm sorry. One way and another I've given you a hard time. I'm not proud of that. I did what I had to for Robin, for my family. I'm – ashamed – of what I did to you. But Frank, I was desperate. I don't expect your forgiveness but I'd like to think you could understand, just a little. You have children of your own. You know what you'd do for them.'

Which, though it wasn't meant to, hit Shapiro hard

204

below the belt. Superintendent Taylor had sabotaged a manslaughter investigation for the sake of his son: David thought his father wouldn't wish him a happy birthday on police time. There must be a way of reconciling public and private duties, but Shapiro wasn't sure either where he would or even where he should resolve a conflict of interests between them.

He put the highest value on his integrity, wouldn't let it go without a struggle for the best cause in the world. At the same time he felt a lack in himself, as a man and as a father, that he couldn't imagine doing for a child of his what Taylor had done.

An echo came to him of what Taylor had said. He started to ask, 'What do you mean, "one way and another"?' But then the phone rang and, after a pause in which the two men eyed one another thoughtfully, Shapiro picked it up.

It was Liz. She said tersely, 'We have a problem.'

7

Donovan blamed himself; with some justice.

From the path beside the house he saw two men going into a green and white marquee. Guessing that the bulky middle-aged man in the army pullover was God's brother and the tall young man his son, Donovan headed towards them, down the slant of the lawn.

Never Boy Scout material, Donovan lacked a formal education in the erection of tents. But even to his untutored eye there was something wrong with this one. Though it was plainly meant to have two poles, at the moment it had only one and that leaned drunkenly. Striped fabric sprawled on the grass like the hide of a badly skinned whale.

Presumably Major Taylor and his nephew hoped to improve matters from the inside. The big man had a heavy wooden mallet, Robin carried a coil of rope over his arm. Actually Donovan didn't care what they were doing as long as he knew where they were. He took up a position at the entrance to the marquee, waiting for Liz to come down from the house.

The sight of him idling there offended the Major's military soul. 'If you've nothing better to do you can help with this.' His voice was a meatier version of God's cultured brogue, developed by bracing cross-country shouts on windswept hillsides.

'Yeah, OK.' He could watch as easily from inside the tent.

'Hold this.' Major Taylor gave him the end of a rope. 'When I tell you, pull.'

Donovan's mistake was to assume they didn't know who he was. He thought the Major had mistaken him for one of the small battalion of hired hands getting the house and garden ready for the wedding.

But soldiers spend their lives surrounded by faces, and it can be vitally important to remember which are which. Ian Taylor knew by name several hundred young men, could identify as friendly forces several hundred more. It gave him an advantage when it came to recognizing half-glimpsed faces. This one he'd seen briefly in the corridor outside his brother's office, but he'd have remembered it if the glance had been even briefer or the face less distinctive. Wedging his shoulder against the teetering tent-pole he said, 'Did my brother send you?'

Wrong-footed, Donovan glanced quickly between the two men. 'Not exactly.'

The big man frowned. 'But you are from his station?' The pole shifted marginally, settled back. He passed the mallet to his nephew, rearranged his strong hands on the pole, dug his heels into the lawn. 'Well, whoever you are, you pull when I push.'

People who train animals for a living argue endlessly about which are the most intelligent, the most amenable, the most responsive. But on the whole they agree which are the most dangerous. Bears have no expression; or rather, their expression doesn't change with their mood. A bear which has, a dozen times a week for three years, trotted round the ring, got on to a barrel, reared up on its back end, taken a bun and got back into line, all with the same ironic smirk on its face, will look exactly the same the day it trots round the ring, gets on to a barrel and rips its trainer's arm off. Lions crouch, elephants flap their ears, but with bears there's no warning.

Donovan fastened his hands to the rope and leaned back, taking the strain. There was no movement that he

207

could feel. He glanced at Robin Taylor but saw no cause for concern: he was between Robin and the entrance, and the young man met his gaze with a friendly smile. Donovan watched the Major, waiting for his signal.

Still smiling, Robin raised the mallet and swung it at Donovan's head.

Donovan never saw it. The first he knew was a bellow as the soldier threw himself forward, shouldering Donovan aside like a charging bull. With a startled yell Donovan went down and the big man swarmed over him.

Landed as aimed, the heavy mallet would have done murder. But when it reached the end of its swing the spot was no longer occupied by Donovan's head, which was down on the grass somewhere wondering which end of the sky had fallen on it, but by Ian Taylor's shoulder.

There was a sickening crunch of bone and the Major let out a soft, agonized grunt. For a moment he stayed where he was, frozen, on his knees with his left arm hanging. Then, quite slowly, he sat down.

Robin went to snatch the weapon up again, careless of the damage he'd already done in his haste to renew his attack. He wore no expression now, not even in his eyes which were dark and quite blank. Bears' eyes.

But Donovan had had a moment to work out what was happening. As the mallet came at him again he lunged for it. Robin didn't fight for it but let go abruptly, kicking out instead at Donovan's face.

There was no comparison between a sledgehammer to the head and a trainer to the jaw. But all the Taylors were substantial men, and it spilled Donovan across the half-erected tent and left him blinking dizzily in a tangle of striped canvas.

A third time Robin lifted the mallet. Speed, luck and surprise had enabled him to dispose of the opposition with remarkable ease: now the initiative was his. He could leave unhindered or remain unobserved. He had plans that meant getting away from here, but enough time to indulge a whim first. He crossed the tent, stepped over Donovan's legs and carefully weighed up the best angle for beating in his skull.

Major Taylor was helpless to intervene. He was conscious, more or less upright with his back against the pole, but he couldn't have risen unaided. He could have shouted, but even if he was heard help could not have reached them in time. He had seconds to stop this, and nothing to do it with except his numbed wits. He croaked, 'Robin, no.'

Robin looked at the injured man, bulky as a downed buffalo. He looked at the implement in his hand as if he'd only just noticed it. He looked at the other man in a dazed sprawl at his feet. Then he looked at the Major again. 'Yes,' he said simply.

It was a time for desperate measures. Ian Taylor had seen men die. He didn't want to watch this one die this way. 'Fire, Robin.'

The boy paused. For a moment something registered in the blank eyes. 'Fire?'

'Flames,' said the soldier, like a waiter tempting a faddy diner. 'Dancing, flickering flames. Lovely roaring flames. All blue and red and gold.'

'Yes,' whispered Robin, his eyes distant.

'They'll catch you if you waste any more time. They'll lock you up where you can't make flames.'

'Flames,' Robin said thoughtfully. 'They *are* lovely.' Still he hesitated, considering the relative merits of two things he very much wanted to do.

Donovan hadn't been knocked out but he had lost his direct line to reality for a minute. His senses had scattered like a flock of startled birds, but now they'd had a bit of a flap round the tent they were settling back on their perches one by one. When enough had come back he remembered what was happening and in sudden panic fought to get control of himself, to get off the ground and away from the maniac with the maul. But his body

209

wouldn't co-operate. Even as he struggled to his hands and knees he knew he couldn't stay ahead of a fit young man with a tenting mallet and the scent of blood.

'It's all right,' a gruff voice said wearily. 'He's gone.'

Donovan whirled round, still on his knees, but all he saw was the injured man propped up against the tent-pole, watching him with heavy eyes. 'Robin?'

'He's gone,' Taylor said again. 'I had to let him go, he'd have killed you if I hadn't. But if you can stagger as far as the door, I think you should raise the alarm. The sooner he's caught, the better.'

'I'm going straight to the Mall.' Liz called Shapiro from the Taylor house. 'I'm sure that's where he's heading. I could use some help; particularly anybody who knows Robin Taylor well enough to spot him in a crowd. I'll know him, and Donovan will, but the uniforms round the door probably won't.'

'I have some bad news about that,' murmured Shapiro. 'The extra men you got Taylor to allocate? He cancelled them when you brought David in for questioning. He said he couldn't justify the overtime when you had the probable culprit. The real reason, of course, was that he knew who'd set the earlier fires and believed there wouldn't be another.'

'Oh, shit,' Liz said feelingly and rang off.

Shapiro put the phone down, thought for a moment, made a decision. 'Come on, James, let's see if we can help. If anybody's going to pick the boy out of a crowd, it's you.'

He was halfway down the corridor before he remembered his own son. He pushed open the interview room door. 'Come on, sunshine, you're in the clear.'

David's eyes gleamed. 'So it was Robin?'

'Yes, it was.'

'You're bringing him in?'

'When we find him.'

210

'You've *lost* him?'

Shapiro explained in a few words, over his shoulder as he headed for his car. 'We're going to the Mall, see if we can spot him before he does any more damage. You left the van at Payne's house, didn't you? Can you make your own way there? I can't spare anyone to take you just now.'

'Stuff the van,' said David indignantly, 'I'm coming with you.' He still had his camera, brandished it as if he'd been drinking.

'It's a public place,' Shapiro allowed tersely. He turned away. 'The same cannot, of course, be said for my car.'

But David fisted a hand in his sleeve and yanked, and Shapiro rounded in surprise. David's face was dark with anger, his eyes afire. 'Don't you turn your back on me! You people brought me here, now you can damn well get me where I need to be. The van or the shopping centre, I don't care which, but you're not leaving me here when I've got a job to do.'

Neither of them was about to give way. Superintendent Taylor said quietly, 'Let him come. I think we owe him that much.' After a moment Shapiro nodded and they hurried out to the yard.

8

It was too late to cancel the opening. It was too late to turn people away in an orderly fashion. The Mall could have been evacuated, but with the crush of people already there the danger was that panic would cause as many casualties as an actual incident.

On the plus side, Robin had left hurriedly and without the chance to take anything with him. If he had money in his pocket he could walk into any garage, say he'd run out of petrol and buy a gallon in a can; but a man carrying a can would be noticed in a crowd of window-shoppers.

There were things they could usefully do, though. Liz had Queen's Street phone a description to the local garages and ask them to delay serving anyone answering it until a car could get there. Two filling stations reported having already served customers who could have been Robin Taylor; or perhaps they were just careless drivers who didn't check their petrol gauges often enough.

Beat officers were instructed to detain anyone carrying a fuel can: even if they didn't find Robin they might establish that both purchasers were *bona fide* so he was still without the means to attack Castle Mall. But whoever bought the petrol had vanished from the streets: by design, or because their cars were no distance from the garages, or because someone took pity and gave them a lift.

The other thing Liz did was explain the situation to the Fire Brigade. Station Officer Silcott agreed to despatch one appliance immediately and have another on stand-by. He couldn't guarantee the Mall priority if an incident occurred elsewhere, but if the worst happened it would save vital minutes.

As time marched resolutely on, what had at first seemed a simple task – finding a sick young man who'd given his keepers the slip, who had a head start of just a few minutes, and who was known by sight to several of the Castlemere police force – began to appear more problematical. The trouble with Robin Taylor was how normal he looked. A policeman's lot would be easier if madmen followed the rules of Gothick fiction and had humps, squinted and were prone to peals of falsetto laughter.

Liz arrived as the sun slid down behind the mock crenellation that formed the roofline of the Castle Mall, decked for the opening in red and yellow pennants. She left Donovan to deploy their forces, went in search of the management. She expected remonstrations at this rude interruption to their expensive festivities from angry men convinced she was wrong. Instead she met a shocked silence. Then one of them asked quietly, 'What do you want us to do?'

It was a relief not having to fight them. 'I can't get these people outside without a panic. Maybe you can. Could you bring the fireworks forward, for instance? If they're out in the open, even if the worst happens at least they'll be able to get away.'

The promotions director was a young man called Peter Voss who'd worked as a disc jockey on local radio. The entertainment was his responsibility, he knew the schedule intimately. 'We can make the announcement, but we can't start for another half-hour. They haven't finished the wiring yet. We didn't think it would be dark enough till after seven.'

'Never mind the God-damned show, Peter,' his colleague said savagely, 'let's just avoid a disaster, yes?'

But the DJ knew what he was talking about. 'Two thousand people aren't going to stand around in a car park for half an hour while we put the finishing touches to a firework display. They'll wait ten minutes, shuffle a bit, then they'll start drifting back inside. By the time we can give them something to look at the Mall will be fuller than it is now.'

Liz had the answer to that. 'In ten minutes I'll have enough people here to close the doors. You get them out and I'll keep them out.'

'Will you send them home?'

Liz chewed her lip. 'I don't know. A thousand cars all leaving at once will snarl up the ring-road for two miles in both directions: if we need that other fire engine, or ambulances, they won't be able to get here.' She thought a moment longer. 'I'll get an assessment from a crowd control expert. In the mean time, is there anything you can do about entertaining them in the car park until the fireworks are ready?'

Voss took a deep breath. 'What the hell, barnstorming's my business. I'll wire a hi-fi into the PA system. If I can get them dancing they'll keep warm while they're waiting for the fireworks and maybe they won't get so ratty. And – prizes. I want a dozen personal stereos, I'll ask them daft questions and give spot prizes. OK?'

Disconcerted at being organized by a twenty-six-year-old DJ, the general manager could only nod.

Liz nodded too, satisfied that it was the best they could do. 'I'll be around. If you need me, call me over the PA – just ask for Liz, no need to alarm the punters. As soon as we find this joker I'll let you know, maybe you can finish the evening with no one any the wiser. And I'll come back to you if we decide to clear the site. I am sorry about this, I know it should have been a big night for you, but—' She gave an apologetic shrug. 'Can you start moving them outside?'

It was never going to be a five-minute job. Mall staff

214

went round the shops telling the proprietors to close, but it had to be done discreetly to avoid a stampede. The story was that the shops would be closed during the outdoor entertainment and open again afterwards. There were complaints from people who'd come here to do some serious shopping at first-day prices, but most went along amiably enough and began wandering towards the exits.

Liz watched from the gallery with a heavy sense of foreboding. It was taking too long: should she risk an announcement over the PA? No, if this lot started to run people would fall and be trampled, and the doors would be jammed and then they'd all be at Robin Taylor's mercy. If he was here. If he'd any sense at all he'd still be running.

He was here. She felt his presence the way people who are allergic to cats know when there's one near by: by the pricking of her skin and the way the hairs stirred at the back of her neck. Days ago, on minimal evidence, she'd known he would come here, and now his shade loomed like the unseen horror in a nightmare. Come on, Peter, she thought desperately, get them out. Tell them they're missing something. Make them hurry!

At Superintendent Taylor's suggestion, he and Shapiro found themselves a spot on the terrace from which they could watch both the main entrance, with shoppers now oozing out of it, and the roped-off section of the car park where the fireworks were being prepared. There was a big black van flashed with red and the legend *Stella Nova* on the side, and men in black jumpsuits hurrying round with boxes. They were working at speed because Liz had explained the situation. She'd also asked them to watch out for someone showing an abnormal interest in their activities.

The Superintendent and his DCI never looked at one another. Their eyes were busy elsewhere. But they continued the conversation begun in Taylor's office.

Shapiro said, 'What did you mean when you said you'd made life difficult for me one way and another?' He'd been pondering that in the odd moments he could spare since the investigation went into turbo with Liz's call.

Taylor said quietly, 'That's something I have to explain. I owe you an apology. Another one. Oh, God, Frank, it's such a mess. I thought I could keep the lid on it. I thought I could protect him without damaging anyone else. I always meant to clear you as soon as he was safe.'

'Clear me?' echoed Shapiro, startled.

Circumstances made it a little easier than it might have been. Talking face to face in the police station would have been immensely difficult. But by now it was almost dark, and they were scanning the floodlit faces for the missing boy, and the illusion of being a two-man island in a sea of strangers created a kind of detached intimacy, almost as if they were talking about two other people.

'I've known about Trevor Foot for nearly a year. I found the photograph and the covering letter in the stationery drawer, as I said, and when I reread the file I understood its significance. I went cold – you can imagine. It was obviously an accident, but it had cost an innocent man seven years in jail. My first instinct, of course, was to call the Chief Constable.

'Then I realized Foot was due for release at any time. I started to wonder if there was anything to be gained by a scandal. A stupid tedious man would get some money he didn't deserve, there'd be a lot of damaging publicity and the investigation would pillory Bob Cassidy in the last months before his retirement: some thanks to a fine station sergeant who on one occasion was overwhelmed by too much happening at once. I put the envelope in the bottom of my desk while I thought about it.

'The longer it sat there, the easier it was to do nothing. If it had been anyone but Foot!' he exclaimed, his voice rising out of its near-monotone in momentary exasperation. 'But we both know the man, he deserved to be in prison for something! And he'd be out any time: it was his own fault he wasn't free already. I suppose I felt the reputation of my police station was worth more than a few months of such a man's time.'

'You left an innocent man in jail? To avoid embarrassment?' Shapiro heard his voice climbing and curbed it before it ran out of control.

Taylor met his gaze with a spark of anger in his eye and a thread of steel in his tone. 'Innocent is a relative term when you're talking about people like that. The fact that it was a bad conviction doesn't necessarily mean it was a miscarriage of justice. I could fill a room with people who believe prison is the very best place Foot could have spent the last eight years. Haven't you noticed how pleasant it's been? No wobbly swastikas on the synagogue walls, no chalk pigs on the mosque, no "Britain for the Brits" graffiti at the job market and the housing office. Filing that photograph in the stationery drawer may have been the best thing Sergeant Cassidy ever did for this town.'

It was the sort of thing that a man might say in the heat of the moment; but no one with any scruples could go on believing it for a year. There had to be more to it than that. Shapiro said quietly, 'You thought you could use it – might need it – sometime? How, why – against whom?' Comprehension jolted him. *Me?*'

Taylor had never been on the uncomfortable side of his DCI's perception before. It was disconcerting. It wasn't important, because he was already committed to a full explanation and he would have got there, but it was disconcerting to find himself beaten to the climax. One of the benefits of being a superintendent is that junior officers don't usually finish your stories.

He let the brief flurry of passion, which was in any event mainly rhetoric, run out of him. He sighed. 'In a way. I suppose I was afraid something like this would happen one day – that I could need some way of keeping you out of action. That picture would be powerful ammunition even after Foot left jail. So I pretended I'd never

217

seen the damned thing; until my present difficulties began.

'You mind, it wasn't till the third fire, at the timber-yard, that I knew Robin was responsible. And you were the investigating officer.' The square shoulders swung as he turned towards Shapiro, trying to pick his face out of the shadows. 'Frank, I was desperate to get you off the case. It's a queer kind of compliment, I know, but that's what it is. I knew you'd work it out. And in spite of everything, he is my son. I thought I could make sure there were no more incidents. All I had to do was keep you out of the way until he went back to Switzerland. Liz Graham's a good detective but she's not in your league. Besides, I could knock all CID sideways by sowing doubts about you. I dug out the photograph, pretended I'd just found it, told HQ and sent you on leave. Then I tipped the *Courier* off so I could claim public concern as the reason for keeping you out of the way.'

He waited for Shapiro to react. But Shapiro said nothing. When the little two-man silence in the sea of noise began to grate Taylor squared his jaw and went on. 'I thought it would be enough. You'd have a couple of weeks off, Robin would go back to the clinic – which I didn't intend he should leave again – then you'd be exonerated. Any flak would come my way, not yours. I wouldn't have done it if there'd been any risk to your career, Frank.'

'That's good to know,' Shapiro said softly.

A man with none of his own, Taylor found humour difficult to deal with. Shapiro's deadpan irony gave him particular problems. A trace of irritation flickered across his face. 'I made one miscalculation. I didn't expect Mrs Graham to get on top of it as soon as she did. She and Donovan are quite a team, aren't they? I had to pull him off the case to slow them down. Not that it made much difference: I think he works harder when he's grounded. Is there a word for that?'

'Bloody-minded?'

'Aye, that's the one,' Taylor nodded lugubriously. 'Well, he's somebody else's problem now.'

'Yes,' agreed Shapiro. After a long moment he said, 'You do realize, James, I can't keep this to myself?'

'Of course not.' Taylor seemed almost to resent the suggestion that he might have expected anything else. 'I knew it could end like this. I hoped not, obviously, but I knew what I was risking. I didn't feel to have any choice – I didn't want my son ending his days in Broadmoor.'

'So you let an innocent man do time instead.' Shapiro shook his head, still finding it hard to believe. 'I'm sorry, James, the rest is semantics – Trevor Foot didn't commit the crime he was imprisoned for, that makes him innocent in every way that matters. And you knew. You didn't wonder about it, you didn't have doubts – you *knew*. And you did nothing.

'For Robin? You love him, I understand that, I have children too; I can imagine doing unwise things, indiscreet things, even stupid things for them. But James, what you did was *criminal*. And it was cruel. You're a senior police officer, for God's sake, you've spent thirty years upholding the law. How could you throw it away like that?'

'I didn't throw it away,' snapped Taylor, stirred to anger by Shapiro's unyielding rectitude. 'I sacrificed it. I sacrificed a bad man to a sick boy. Not even that: one year in the life of a bad man. I couldn't have kept Foot out of jail, I could only have expedited his release. And for that I'd have had to turn my back on my own child. I was the only one who could help him, Frank. Was it so very great a price to pay?'

'Foot's freedom?' mused Shapiro. 'Your career. And this?' His gaze circled the crowds milling round them. 'Any one of them, James. Any one of them was too high a price.'

'I suppose if it'd been *your* son you'd have let the law take its course?' It was meant as sarcasm; since Shapiro would, it came across as nastier than that. 'Well, that makes you a grand policeman, Frank; but I don't envy what it says about you as a father.'

Stung, Shapiro retorted, 'Being a father isn't what I'm paid for. I do that on my own time. If I thought I couldn't do my job *and* care for my children without a conflict of interest my resignation would be on your desk at close of play.' He added, a cheap barb that he immediately regretted and wouldn't have loosed except that Taylor had got under his skin, 'At least, on somebody's.'

But they were both upset and he didn't have a monopoly on cheap shots. 'You're sure of that?' asked Taylor. 'That you'd have sent your resignation to me? Or would it have gone to David?'

Shapiro recoiled as if he'd been slapped. But he managed not to respond in kind: if they kept this up they'd end up brawling in the car park. He let the anger go in a sigh. 'There's never only one way, James. If there was there'd be no such thing as free will and without that no right and wrong. I believe – dear God, I thought we all believed – in absolute wrong. What you did was wrong, not because of who Foot is but because of who you are. Not because he spent time in prison that he shouldn't have done, but because you should have got him free and didn't. That's what matters. Not Bob Cassidy's mistake; not Robin's illness; not even the fact that I couldn't tell the difference between an innocent man and a guilty one. The fact that you abused the power you were entrusted with. I understand your anguish. I don't begin to understand your actions.'

'And if you're very, very lucky,' Taylor said quietly, 'perhaps you never will.'

There was nothing more to say. It wasn't an argument that was capable of resolution. He'd done it for love. Cool, precise, fastidious Superintendent James Taylor had laid down his career, his standing in the community, probably his freedom, for something as intangible as love. It could be neither attacked nor defended on rational grounds. It was worth it if he thought it was.

They stood on the raised terrace, leaning on the railing, watching the crowd in the car park slowly grow, listening to the heavy beat and mindless prattle coming over the public address system, watching the men in black prepare their pretty, seductive display, watching people stroll out of the main entrance with bulging shopping bags, with fractious children, with pushchairs, with no idea of the danger they might be in.

After a while Taylor gave voice to a thought that had occurred to Shapiro too; also Liz, and Donovan and probably every other police officer there that evening. 'What if he's gone somewhere else?'

9

Even David Shapiro, who was not a police officer, could see that the more manpower was concentrated here, the less there was patrolling the quiet streets and shining torches at the shuttered windows of shops. 'What if he's gone somewhere else?'

Donovan shrugged. 'Then we'll be out another warehouse by morning. But at least it won't have been packed with people.'

They weren't watching the shoppers, they'd joined them, forging salmon-wise against the stream leaving the Mall until they were bringing up the rear. That way, Donovan reasoned, if something started in the heart of the building he wouldn't have to fight his way through a panic-stricken mob to reach anywhere he could do some good. Also, he wasn't above a little threatening behaviour to encourage tardy customers to move out and shops to close as they'd been asked.

David stayed with him because experience, of which he had some, and instinct, of which he had more, both told him Donovan was the sort of person things happened around. If Robin Taylor was here, and if he started a fire, Donovan would be nearest.

As they shuffled towards the main entrance, leaving empty halls behind, jangly music and Peter Voss's manic chatter washed in at them. 'Here's another question you never thought to ask yourself. What's green and hairy and crosses water at twenty-five knots? How about you, madam, you look like you could do with a bit of rhythm in your life. For the last word in personal stereos, what's green and hairy and ... What do you mean, your husband on waterskis? I always thought it was a gooseberry with an outboard engine, but I'm not going to call you a liar. Here, catch ...'

'He's gone somewhere else,' said David with conviction. 'Or he's making a run for it. He knows you're on to him, why would he hang around when he could be putting miles behind him? He'd have to be—' He stopped.

'Yeah,' grunted Donovan with some irony. 'Crazy.'

His eyes roved left and right over the people moving ahead of him, still hoping to glimpse the man they sought. But the more time passed the more hope faded. If he was here he'd got in unseen, could leave the same way; and if he wasn't already inside he was too late. Either the scale of the police response had frightened him off or Inspector Graham had been wrong all along. If it turned out Robin Taylor had never been within five miles of the place she'd be going round red faced for days.

David's thoughts had been running on different lines. 'People's frigging families,' he said with feeling. 'As if people can't fuck themselves up without help.'

Donovan glanced at him. 'God? It wasn't Robin fucked him up, it was his own inability to draw the line between private interest and professional duty.'

'So he deserves this?' demanded David. 'His career shattered because his son's a psychopath? I think I'm a callous sod sometimes, Donovan, but next to you I'm an amateur.'

Donovan replied with a wolfish smile. 'Next to me, kid, most people are amateurs. Taylor hit a problem he couldn't hack, and the way he dealt with it put lives in danger. You can sympathize, but you can't say he's a fit person to run a police station. Sooner or later he'd hit another problem he couldn't hack.'

'You think it takes a man incapable of error to be a

police chief? There are going to be a lot of vacancies.' David gave a dark chuckle. 'Maybe my dad could fill one of them. Whatever his failings, he'd never have made Taylor's mistake.'

Donovan looked away and shook his head. 'You can't forgive him that, can you? For making a better policeman than a father.'

'I can live with it,' David said stiffly. 'He was the one with unrealistic expectations. He was disappointed in me from further back than I can remember. You've no idea how hard I tried not to let him down. I sweated blood for him, but it was never enough. There was always something I could have done better, or differently, or not done at all that would have kept that look of weary resignation out of his eyes. He crucified me. And do you know the worst part? I don't think he even knew he was doing it.'

Donovan shrugged. 'I think you've both got unrealistic expectations. Fathers and sons always gut one another: that's how the system works. There's nothing unique about you and the Chief.'

David broke his stride, surprised. 'Then what are you supposed to do?'

'Get through, somehow,' said Donovan. 'This idea that fathers and sons should get along – it's a human fallacy. 'Most everything else on earth takes pains to keep generations of males apart. Loads of fathers draw the line at conception; some hang around just long enough to provide a bit of food. It's only us thinks you can't enjoy a good hump without being responsible for the consequences until one of you dies.'

The woman in front of them turned a startled face in his direction.

David grinned. 'So—?'

'So you don't owe one another. If he gets up your nose, walk away.'

'I don't want to walk away.' David seemed surprised to hear himself say it. 'I admire him. I just wish he was easier to like.'

224

'Why?'

'*Why?*' came the exasperated echo. 'Because it would be . . . nice. Because you should like decent people. Don't you like him?'

Donovan thought for a minute, then shook his head. 'I – always respected him.' When he finally learned that he'd been both right and wrong, that someone had concealed the photograph and that it wasn't Frank Shapiro, it would be like a ton weight lifted off his mind. 'I'm not sure I like anybody.'

David started to laugh. 'Why the hell am I listening to you? I need the advice of an emotional cripple like a steeplejack needs an aqualung.'

Donovan gave a saturnine grin and didn't deny it.

The woman in front turned to them again. 'What *is* that?'

'Sorry?' said Donovan blankly.

'I can smell something,' said the woman, a puzzled and slightly anxious frown creasing her forehead. 'I'm sure I can smell smoke.'

Even though she was half expecting it, the fire alarm sent such a jolt through Liz that for a second she froze. She was up on the gallery again, leaning on the parapet, scanning the dawdling crowd; at the sound her hands clutched the rail so fiercely that her knuckles turned white.

The soprano two-tone came from a small boutique just off the main hall. Five avenues radiated out in a star shape, with bigger enterprises towards the far ends and a Village Green of small shops at the heart of the complex. The boutique was called Maid Marion's and there was a lot of green in the window. Behind the window display there was some wispy smoke. A girl came rushing out of the door and stood in the concourse crying, 'Can someone help me . . .?'

Donovan was nearest and sprinted past her into the shop. David Shapiro was at his heels, the camera already to his face.

Heads turned all over the Mall as the shoppers tried to see what was happening and if it was part of the festivities. People called their children to them. Some quickened their steps towards the exit, others hovered where they were and stood on tiptoe, craning.

From the top of the stairs Liz raised her voice over the interrogative hum. 'There's nothing to worry about but it would help if everyone would leave now, in case we need to run a hose through here.'

That was when the second alarm went off, in a china shop across the Village Green. The hum turned to an anxious hubbub with voices raised shrilly above it. There was a general determined movement towards the doors.

Sirens wailed in stereo in adjacent shops near the exit. The crowd stopped in its tracks and milled uncertainly, fire behind them and fire ahead, unable to quantify the danger, afraid of moving into burgeoning flame and exploding plate-glass.

The speed with which he reached it enabled Donovan to smother the little fire in the boutique before the evidence of how it started was destroyed. He did what the girl should have done: hauled the stock off the rails and trampled the burning dresses under other goods till the flames asphyxiated. Of course, he didn't have to answer to the girl's Aunty Marion, who'd selected every item with the loving care of someone fulfilling a life's ambition.

When he dug out the worst-affected garment and searched for the remnants of a pocket, he saw how it was done. Robin Taylor had needed neither time nor facilities to prepare an incendiary device. He'd walked into a corner shop and bought a few matchboxes with the small change in his pockets, and started a separate fire with each.

Donovan had played the same trick in Glencurran at a time – he must have been very young – when it still seemed funny to make people think they were being fire-bombed. You wedged matches in the lid of the box so that when you lit the first one it burned down and lit others which lit others which finally lit the rest in a powerful little flare hot enough to start a fire.

By arranging the matches in different ways you could delay combustion for anything up to a minute. Long enough, in the Glencurran of twenty years ago, for the village's nastier little boys to take cover and watch the results from a safe distance. And long enough today, in the noise and bustle of a new shopping centre, for a madman to be strolling round leaving his little packages where they could smoulder unnoticed for a while before bursting into terrifying life.

At the china shop he'd left one in a box of shredded paper packaging, at the stationery shop near the entrance he'd put one behind a pile of jigsaws and in the haberdasher's next door he'd secreted it among the fancy trimmings. Although he hadn't been able to pursue his hobby recently he hadn't forgotten the governing principles. He still got an itch at the back of his nose when he looked at something seriously flammable.

As Donovan stamped out the last embers among the latest fashions he heard the consternation outside: the crash of glass, the milling cattle sounds, the clatter of feet as they hurried back towards him. 'God damn!' He reached the boutique door as the knot of people swarmed past.

There might have been thirty of them, men, women and children, not yet a stampede because it wasn't panic driving them but a wholly rational desire to find a safe exit. They were making haste but not yet running blindly. The women still had hold of their children's hands, the men of their wives'. One young woman with a pushchair stooped to rescue a faded teddy ejected by the conveyance's other occupant.

Donovan took a moment to look around. The situation had changed while he was inside the shop, continued to develop even as he watched. Perhaps Robin Taylor had

had more to work his mischief with than just matchboxes – there were still two cans of petrol unaccounted for – or perhaps it was his skill with them that was paying dividends. Across the concourse the china shop was ablaze, pewter smoke wreathing in the window and flames belching from the open door. The tinsel and crêpe paper and Chinese lanterns with which the halls had been decorated made a conduit along which the fire could spread: already the paper and plastic strands were dripping flame into adjoining doorways.

There was also smoke and a little flame from the two shops flanking the main entrance, and a new conflagration starting further back into the building: a bad one to judge from the amount of dense black smoke rolling into the hallway. The situation wasn't a disaster yet but it was getting seriously unpleasant.

Donovan raised his voice above the hubbub and the clatter of feet, bringing the running people to an uncertain halt. 'Where the hell do you think you're going?'

The woman with the pushchair looked at him quickly, recognizing the note of authority, her eyes full of fear and expectation. 'There's a fire. At the entrance, we can't get past. There must be another way out—?'

There was, of course; there were a number, and Donovan knew where they were. It was the first thing Liz had asked when they arrived. But the closest was a lot further than the main door, and also a lot narrower: if one of Robin Taylor's little packages flared up before they got there they could find themselves trapped. If one exploded as they got there they could trample one another fighting to get through.

He looked again towards the entrance. Flames were lapping now through the broken glass of both shop windows but the hall was wide, there was room to pass. As he watched another group of people, obeying the quieter authority of his inspector in the way people tended to, even himself if he didn't keep his wits about him, took their courage in their hands and ran the gauntlet, reaching the safety of the open door to a muted chorus of cheers.

There was no doubt in Donovan's mind that his people should leave the same way. Half a minute and they could be outside. The fire wasn't going to run out of control in that time: the fire crew already had a hose run out on the far side. It had to be safer than heading into the heart of a burning building in the hope that they could reach a back exit.

So he lied. 'There isn't. The way in is the way out. Ach, it's only a little fire, we'll get past easy enough.'

He drove them like a Border collie driving sheep, anticipating where they might scatter and turn back and making sure that the first thing they saw when they glanced behind was him. He couldn't have stopped a determined mutiny. But as long as he seemed to know what he was doing, as long as the low monotone of his voice and the deliberate movements of his long body bespoke confidence, they would do as he said. As long as he seemed to be in control he was in control.

He moved them quickly towards the exit, and the only moment of drama was when David took one close-up too many of the policeman's hawkish profile, contrasting its grim determination with the amorphous shades of anxiety around him, and Donovan picked him up by his shirt-front and said very quietly into his face, 'Stop it.'

When they reached the haberdasher's, its window belching a healthy adolescent blaze, the flock slowed and then stopped, looking from Donovan to the fire and back as if wondering which was the most dangerous.

He pushed through to where the front rank was holding up the advance. Irritation barred his voice. 'For pity's sake, you could drive a petrol-tanker through there! Take a run at it and you'll be through before you feel the heat.'

He thought about giving a demonstration but he was afraid that if he left them, even for a moment, they'd turn away and take their chances in the smoky labyrinth of the Mall. He pushed David through the shuffling knot. 'Go on, show them.'

David Shapiro had seen many fires in the last year, all of them at close quarters, most of them bigger than this. Familiarity had bred affection rather than contempt, but it had also taught him how much he could get away with. How close he could dance to the painted girl without ending up in her embrace. He knew Donovan was right: the flames weren't suddenly going to leap across the hallway incinerating everything in their path. This fire would do a lot more chest-beating before it went ape. He didn't run past, he sauntered.

'See?' said Donovan. 'Come on now, let's do it.'

Still they hesitated. 'What if—?'

'It won't,' he said forcibly. 'Now, are you going or do I have to throw you?'

'What about this?' someone said. A small fire-extinguisher was waved in the air.

It wasn't part of the shopping centre's fire precautions; perhaps someone had bought it in the car accessories shop across the Village Green. It wasn't big enough to make any impact – except on their morale, and right now it was lack of morale that was delaying their escape. Donovan nodded. 'OK. Aim at the base of the fire, inside the window. Do it now.'

He didn't wait to see the results. He knew they would be minimal. But there would be a moment before these people realized that when he could herd them to safety; he edged himself into the best position to do it and filled his lungs like John Wayne starting a cattle-drive.

But as he did so his eye recorded, as a kind of visual echo, something that didn't fit, and urgent as the other demands on his attention were he couldn't leave it alone until he pinned it down. Even then he didn't know what it meant. Someone smiling. Not the woman handling the fire extinguisher, the man behind who'd passed it to her. Smiling against the backdrop of the flames.

From a vague unfocused sense of something not right Donovan went to a full-blown appreciation of what was wrong at a speed defying the laws of physics. In all the wide world he knew only two men capable of smiling at such a time, and one of them had just strolled nonchalantly past the blazing shops. The other was Robin Taylor, who'd been missing quite long enough to buy a small domestic extinguisher and replace its contents with petrol from the can he'd bought at an unsuspecting garage.

He lunged forward, throwing people aside in his haste to reach the woman with the extinguisher. Even as he dived for her he yelled, 'Don't use—'

But it was too late. She was doing her best for everyone and she didn't waste any time. She read the instructions once and carried them out to the letter. A powerful little jet sprang from the extinguisher as Donovan reached for her arm.

Fed by petrol under pressure, the playful blaze turned in the wink of an eye to a great golden beast that leapt ravening from its lair straight at the gathered people, its flickering hugeness filling the exit they had hesitated too long to take. There was one shrill scream from the woman closest to it before the beast got her by the throat. After that there were shouts and screams everywhere, but none of them rose above the roaring of the fire.

10

Donovan was hit by three things in rapid succession – blinding light, searing heat and the body of the woman thrown back by the explosive energy of the flare. He staggered, lost his footing and went down, and the fire rolled over him.

Liz, watching from the door, unaware until a split second before of any reason this group shouldn't make their way to safety as hers had done, saw the great gout of flame leap from the window and envelop the two figures closest. She saw Donovan lurch back with the screaming woman in his arms, saw him begin to fall; then like a billow of yellow silk in a Chinese pageant the fire enfolded him.

She cried out – not his name: 'Sergeant—!' Then big men in boots and oilskins shouldered her aside and a jet of hard water flew to meet the jet of flame.

As the hose swept the fire aside like a broom clearing leaves from a path the people who had shrunk back from it screaming saw salvation. Firemen came in under the hose to guide them out but they didn't wait, charging the stream to reach the safety of oilskin arms. Liz had to fight her way through them to follow the firemen into the Mall.

Though they knew who she was they shouldn't have let her pass; but in the chaos those who had the authority to stop her didn't see her and those who saw her didn't think she'd take no for an answer. She reached the casualties three strides behind Station Officer Silcott.

For a moment she not only couldn't tell if they were alive, she couldn't tell which limbs were whose. All she could make out was a shapeless huddle on the floor, burned flesh glistening through charred cloth, an island of human wreckage in a fresh-water sea one centimetre deep. She bent and reached out but dared not touch them. 'Oh, dear God . . .'

Silcott spared her a moment's kindness in his glance. 'It may not be as bad as it looks.'

Paramedics untangled the clasped bodies. Donovan surfaced to a sensation like having his fingers broken. The woman had spun against him and automatically he'd thrown his arm protectively around her. Now it was locked there, the fingers clenched on her shoulder. In fact she'd protected him. That arm was the only part of him directly exposed to the flash, and the skin was seared from knuckles to biceps, shiny red and black where his sleeve had charred into it. Otherwise he was barely touched. The woman, by contrast, was burned the length of her back and legs, the only undamaged skin a diagonal band under Donovan's arm.

'She's an emergency,' the paramedic rapped out tersely. 'He's just going to be bloody sore.'

They stretchered the woman out but the policeman was hauled to his feet and steered out more or less under his own power. Liz went with him, his good arm round her shoulders and hers round his waist, talking to him steadily. For a minute shock held him in limbo, with no clear idea what had happened or even if he'd been hurt. He looked at her vaguely as if he wasn't sure who she was. Then all at once she saw the slack muscles of his face firm and then clench as the pain of his arm got through to him.

By the time they got outside the woman was on board and the ambulance ready to leave, its lamp flashing to clear an exit. There was just time for Shapiro to push through the crowd, stick his head in at the open door and demand, 'Is he going to be all right?' And for Donovan to grit through his teeth, 'Yeah – except that he's lost his voice.' Then the paramedics slammed the door and the ambulance left with its siren wailing.

Liz and Shapiro used the space where it had been to talk. Some of what had gone before she had inferred, some of it she'd had thrown at her in hasty snatches just comprehensive enough for her to take the required actions. This was her first chance to hear it all, in detail and in sequence, and though it was a shocking story she was less surprised than she might have been. Less surprised than Shapiro had been; and perhaps more understanding.

Around them as they talked, rocking like an ocean, unsure what to do or where to go next, relieved to be safely outside but reluctant to turn their backs on the spectacle, two thousand people crowded the car park and leaned first towards the main entrance where the fire engine was pumping water by the ton into the burning building, then the other way to make sure they weren't missing the fireworks.

Peter Voss had wound up his act by now: everyone was out, the danger of mass panic was over, what they'd feared had happened but the situation was under control. At intervals Voss asked everyone to go home now, they'd do the fireworks another night, but there was little hope in his voice. Soon local radio would carry a bulletin; then, far from dispersing, the crowd would grow. Because the opening of a shopping centre is only a PR event, but nobody wants to miss a good fire.

'Oh, God,' sighed Shapiro dispiritedly, 'what a shambles. Donovan hurt; that poor girl terribly hurt; the damage here's going to run into hundreds of thousands; all because of one mad boy with a fire fetish. Do we know where he is?'

Liz nodded at the entrance, hoses leading in and smoke wreathing out. 'He was in there. Five, six minutes ago he was right there, outside the haberdasher's. I didn't see him leave. Unless we missed him, he's still in there.'

From outside it was hard to judge whether the fire was still spreading or if the firemen had mastered it. The rosy light flickering within said there were flames yet to be extinguished but not how big a task that would be.

'I'd better tell Silcott.' Shapiro headed into the entrance where the Station Officer was directing operations.

While Shapiro was talking to Silcott Liz let her gaze travel over the crowd; not expecting to see the missing man, mostly out of habit. Uniform were moving people away from the building a few yards at a time and widening the corridor for the emergency services. As she watched a second fire engine did a handbrake turn off the ring road and surged through the crowd, everything on it that could flash or wail doing so.

David Shapiro arrived out of the bedlam without warning or greeting; one moment there was no sign of him, the next he was standing beside her, wiping his lens with a tissue as if he'd been there all along. 'There's a rear exit still open,' he said casually. 'Are you coming?'

She stared as if he'd offered her a caterpillar sandwich. 'Until those nice men in the Dayglo oilskins tell me it's safe, I'm not even peeping through a window.'

He shrugged. 'Suit yourself. I just thought Robin might leave that way. Still, you know your job.' He padded off along the side of the building, the camera on his chest like a badge of office.

Liz hesitated, drew a breath to call her chief. Then she let it go in a muttered profanity and trotted after his son. There were two reasons. One was that he was right, the exit should be watched, but taking officers out of the cordon could weaken it fatally. The other was that she suspected David meant to enter the building, his sights set on a climax for his portfolio, and if she asked him not to he just might not but if his father asked he would. David Shapiro was a young man who could literally die of obstinacy.

The rear of the great pentagonal building ran parallel to the site boundary, only the unloading bays and room to swing a juggernaut between it and the fence. With the bulk of the building between them and all the activity the area was dark. Liz found it hard to maintain her focus on the shadow that was David Shapiro moving among the other shadows; when he stopped she almost walked into him. 'There.'

It wasn't the only fire exit at the rear of the building. The reason David had come here, Liz realized, was not because Robin Taylor was more likely to use this one than the others but because it suited his own purpose better. Emergency exits are designed to be opened from the inside, but there had been much coming and going earlier in the evening, putting the finishing touches to the opening displays, and the door had been wedged open. It gave on to a corridor, and the corridor was also dark but at the end danced a faint roseate glow.

David checked his camera, confident as a blind man of the feel of the settings, and moved towards the opening. Liz put her hand on his arm. 'That wasn't part of the deal.'

She felt him looking at her. 'There was no deal.' His tone was ambivalent: she heard wariness and elation, challenge and humour weaving through it. The feelings of a sportsman before a big game.

'You'll get me sacked,' she said, keeping her voice light. 'And if Station Officer Silcott finds you prancing about in there while his men are trying to work he'll attach you to his hose with a jubilee clip.'

David snorted with laughter. 'Tell you what. In the interests of protecting your employment, and saving me from a close encounter with a jubilee clip, I'll just go to the end of the corridor and shoot what I can see from there. OK?'

It wouldn't have been all right if she'd believed him, and she didn't believe him. But as she opened her mouth to say so, glancing over his shoulder she suddenly saw the quality of light inside the corridor diminish. It might have been the fires dying back but seemed too abrupt, more as if something had passed in front of the light. Her body went as still as a pointer's. After a moment David realized why their argument had ended in a sudden silence and turned to watch too.

Someone was moving in the corridor. Not a fireman, the outline of the helmet was missing and the figure moved too freely for someone in boots and oilskins. At the same time there was indecision in the way it took a few paces towards the door, turned and hovered a moment watching the fires, turned again and made once more for the open air.

'It's him, isn't it?' whispered David.

'I think so.'

They whispered because unless he heard them Robin Taylor couldn't know they were there. They could see him because he was silhouetted against the glow, but behind them was only more darkness.

In spite of which Liz knew what David was doing as if the small movements of his hands were taking place in the beam of an arc-lamp. 'Use that camera,' she breathed, 'and I'll put it where the next picture it takes will make medical history.' His hands returned to his sides.

They inched apart, afraid that even in the dark Robin would see them as he reached the door. Now he was ready to leave, it seemed, because he didn't look back again but came directly at them, not hurrying but not hesitating either. It was clear from the rhythm of his stride that he had no idea he was observed.

Liz wished now she'd risked taking men from crowd control. But it was already too late: if she called for help she'd drive him back into the building, if she ran for help they'd lose him in the dark, if she sent David the reinforcements would be too long coming and she'd have to face him alone. She hadn't forgotten the damage he'd inflicted on his uncle and Donovan, each of them stronger than she was. Her only real weapon was surprise; all her ingenuity now was bent to using it.

She stooped carefully, eyes glued to the movement in the corridor, and lifted the half-brick wedging the door, keeping it open with her hand. Kicking the brick aside would have made a noise; the other advantage was that if need be she could thump him with it. Carrying unauthorized weapons was the quickest way Liz knew for a detective inspector to get back on points duty, but making use of what came to hand in an emergency was intelligent policing.

It wasn't much of a plan, but what she intended to do was wait until he stepped outside then let the door close behind him, identify herself and arrest him. She thought he would either try to return to the building, wasting time and energy trying to open a door with no outside handle, or make a break for the perimeter fence. Either way she'd tackle him from behind, the safest way with a dangerous man. Then she'd yell her head off and hope help would come before he could struggle free and beat her face in.

Of course, there was David. She didn't know how much she could rely on him. He was smaller than her and he hadn't done training courses in subduing violent criminals but he was better than nothing. As a last resort he could dazzle Robin with his flashgun.

She never knew what alerted him. She made neither sound nor movement to betray her presence, and she didn't believe that David did. But four or five paces from the door Robin suddenly became uneasy. He slowed, glanced behind him, tipped his head on one side and seemed to peer into the darkness outside. She froze where she stood, three-quarters behind the door; only her hand and half her face would have been visible had there been light to see, and she didn't dare shift those for fear that the movement would confirm his suspicion. She held her breath in case he was doing the same in order to listen.

For what seemed a long time, and probably was a

238

couple of minutes, none of the three of them moved. They breathed, when they had to, through their mouths. David remained invisible against the wall; Liz concentrated on keeping the door still. The faceless shade that was Robin Taylor remained balanced on the balls of its feet, its hands lightly spread, ready to dance back at any moment. Only the fact that he wasn't sure, that he felt the presence of another person but saw and heard nothing, kept him there.

At last he seemed reassured by the continued silence, the dearth of movement. The shape of him relaxed a fraction, the hands coming down, the weight dropping into the feet. He took a step towards the door.

And it was at that moment, with the man she sought almost within her grasp and still unaware of her, that the fires which continued to burn inside the Mall got a sudden new impetus from somewhere and flared up behind him, casting a gout of rosy light the length of the dark corridor. It was only for a second but it was enough. It showed him the half-open door, the hand holding it, the face peering round it. He knew he'd been right when he sensed a waiting presence.

What he didn't know was whether it was one person or a posse waiting for him. If he'd known it was only one woman detective with the dubious support of a magazine photographer he might have come on. Probably he could have flattened them both and been over the perimeter fence before anyone could stop him. But he had no reason to suppose it was a cut-price reception committee. He thought if he came out he'd be caught.

He thought if he went back, back into the element he loved and understood as no one else in his experience did, he would be safe. It wasn't an act of despair, choosing suicide as the least undignified way out. The fire was his creation, his child and his beauty, and he believed he could pass through it unharmed. He turned from the darkness and ran to its flaming heart because he believed he would be safe there and any who tried to pursue him would not.

There was no further point in concealment. Liz sprang into the doorway crying, 'Robin, come back,' at the top of her voice. But there was no reply, only the swift tattoo of his running feet. 'God *damn*!' she exclaimed in fury and despair.

Robin Taylor had done many odd things, many obscene things, many downright insane things. But this was his first miscalculation: to think he was the only one who knew his way around fires as other men know their lovers' bodies. David Shapiro was another. He passed Liz calmly, without hesitation or fuss. 'I'll get him.'

Liz stared at him aghast. 'You're not going in there!'

He thought about it for a moment, then nodded. 'Yes, I am.' And he did.

11

When he reached the end of the corridor David understood why Robin Taylor decided to leave when he did. Even for a pyromaniac the Mall had become too hot to handle.

David was surprised how much progress the blaze had made against the combined efforts of the sprinkler system and the firemen's hoses. It should have been dying back by now. He'd seen too many fires to expect instant results on anything bigger than an overheated chip-pan, but all the water pouring on to it should have had some effect. The only explanation he could think of was that as the firemen battled their way in from the front Robin was retreating behind the flames, helping them to spread, thinking they'd cover his retreat. He'd tried to leave now because there was almost nowhere left to retreat to.

The open space of the Village Green was a cauldron, flames shooting into the five-sided lantern above. The roar beat at his ears, incandescence seared his eyes. When he remembered to breathe again the hot wind caught in his throat like raw spirit.

Then there was the smoke. Great black coils of the stuff climbed on the backs of the flames to leap in writhing fury against the ceiling; denied escape, they turned over in a madness of frustration and flung out all ways from the fire that spawned them. On the way down from the ceiling black smoke met plumes of white steam and the two coiled together like lovers, or predator and prey.

241

And the hot wind smelled of everything that had burned in that great burning building: acrid chemical smells and sweet pungent smells, and oily ones, and others so foul they scourged the eyes and thickened the tongue and it didn't take an expert to know there were lethal toxins in the dense cocktail.

Watching it, listening to it, even smelling it filled him with a kind of wonder. The power of it beat down on him, awesome and terrible; yet at the same time he was somehow part of that power, revelling in it. He was in a place few men had ventured, few dared go, and there was a thrill of pride in that which was fundamental to him. What he had done, what he was doing now, helped define what he was. Combat pilots, trapeze artists, bull fighters, deep-sea divers: he danced with them on the filamentary wire over the pit, only the lightness of his feet and the steadiness of his nerve between him and the agony of destruction. No wonder people didn't understand him. What he was made no sense, except to others who chose to defy death as a way of life.

Men like Robin Taylor, he thought then. Men who let the power and the beauty enter their souls and drive them mad. A fear stirred in him that was not the fear of the flames. Is that where I'm going? My inevitable end, when the addiction takes over and I can't do without the thing that's going to kill me? Thus far he had believed himself here by choice, that the risks he took were calculated and purposeful and, even if it wasn't always apparent, he controlled his own actions and to a great extent his own destiny. But what if he was wrong? What if it was the compulsion controlling him all along?

A hand closed on his wrist and he started guiltily, reaching for the camera. It was his touchstone, his passport to an arcane world he could not have travelled without it; yet this close to the best pictures of his life it hung neglected on his chest, a mere decoration, like tinsel medals on a carnival general. His fingers fumbled with it while his brain reeled with insight like a slap.

242

Liz said flatly, 'You're not going any further. He's gone, David. You can't save him. I'm damned if I'll let you go too.' Her voice rasped with the fumes and she had to shout over the bellow of the flames. Even so there was an audible tremor running through it.

David shook his head. 'No. This is as far as I go.' His voice was ambivalent, as if he were conducting some other conversation, not the one with her.

She sensed a hidden agenda; but whatever the question, the answer seemed to bring him back to her. For a moment, before she found the grit to hurry after him, she'd thought he would keep on walking past the end of the corridor, walk into the flames as if he believed himself invulnerable, vanish into the blinding light and never emerge. But that danger had passed, even if she didn't know quite how. Relief left her absurdly light-headed for someone in a burning building.

She cleared her throat. 'What about your pictures?'

His hands manipulated the settings automatically. He had the camera halfway to his face; then he lowered it again. 'I've got everything I need. Let's get out while we can.' He smiled at her, and in the glow of the flames his face was a little drawn and smudged with smoke but free of the passion that had driven him, as if he'd found cathar- sis in the very heart of the flames. There was even a little self-mocking irony in his eyes. Liz thought, He's back. Wherever it is he's been, he's back. She nodded and cast a last glance into the inferno before leaving.

That was when they saw him. Simultaneously: if only Liz had spotted the figure through the flames she would have said nothing until they were outside and she could tell the firemen. But David saw him too, and they traded a quick glance that confirmed neither had imagined it.

'Oh, shit,' said David wearily.

Liz fisted her hand in his sleeve. 'This is not your prob- lem. You shouldn't even be here. Just across the hall there are men with the equipment and the know-how to get him out.'

'And they don't know where he is, and we do,' said David. 'By the time we tell them he'll be somewhere else, or he'll be dead.'

'He started this!' she cried. 'He's not worth risking your life for.'

David looked straight at her and smiled again. 'A minute ago I was going to walk in there for the sake of some photographs. I'm not going to walk away and let a man burn.'

'If you can find your way in, he can find his way out!'

He explained it carefully, as if she were a simpleton. 'Inspector, he's not responsible. Not for what he's done, and not for his actions now. He can't be punished, he needs looking after; and right here and now I'm the only one who can do it.'

Liz nodded slowly. 'Your father's right about you. He said you always had more guts than you knew what to do with.'

'Did he?' David mulled that over as if it surprised him. Then he shook himself. 'Oh well, this won't bath no babies. Wish me luck?'

'I can do better than that,' she said, pointing. 'Look.'

'Where?' He followed her finger, turning away.

Behind his back Liz swung the half-brick in her left hand, gritting her teeth because she despised violence but this time, in these precise circumstances, she knew the half-brick would serve where any amount of well-honed argument would not.

The horrid sound of a fistful of masonry colliding with a man's skull made her wince. But it had the desired effect. For an instant she thought she hadn't hit him hard enough, he only staggered slightly and began to turn back to her, his hands going to his head, his face shocked. Then as she watched, ready to do it again if need be, his eyes rolled up, his knees sagged and he slid bonelessly to the floor.

Liz stood over him, more protective than triumphant,

244

for a moment while she waited for her heart to steady. She looked into the fire dancing at the end of the corridor. She said to herself, aloud, 'I suppose the proper thing to do is get in there, find the idiot boy who started this and haul him out before allowing a single feminine tear to drop into my lilac-scented handkerchief.' The flames leapt and roared encouragement.

She turned her back on them. 'Bugger that.' Bending, she took one of David Shapiro's slack hands in her own and dragged him towards the open air; and if, as she reached the door, with the blood pounding in her ears and the sweat of effort on her brow, she heard the thunder of the flames split for a few seconds by the screams of a live thing in mortal torment, she gave no outward sign of it.

Shapiro went in the ambulance, cradling his son's bloody head in his lap, tears in the seams of his cheeks. Beyond a three-line explanation of the facts Liz had not discussed with him what happened. There would be time later to review all that had been done and judge in the light of the outcome which of their decisions and actions had been the right ones. If he was unhappy with her actions she'd find out then.

In her own mind she was sure she'd done the only thing possible. If Shapiro didn't know that already he would by the time David's head was stitched and his concussion fading, and he'd had space to reflect on the other ways this could have ended.

He hadn't wanted to leave the scene with the emergency still in progress but Liz insisted. 'Silcott needs no advice from you on how to bring a fire under control. There's no chance now of making someone amenable. Uniform have the crowd in hand, and anything else that comes up I'll deal with. Go with him, Frank, be there when he wakes up. For once, put your duty second.' So he'd gone.

There remained Superintendent Taylor. His actions too awaited judgement on another day; but the man was not in any conventional sense a criminal and there was no chance of him turning fugitive. Liz knew that if she did nothing he would remain at the Mall for as long as he thought there was anything to wait for; then he'd return to his office and prepare for a smooth handover of the power he had abused.

Before that she wanted to see him, to express her sympathy and put certain things on record. If she didn't do it now there mightn't be another opportunity.

She found him sitting in the back of a squad car parked by the main entrance, watching the continuing activities of the firefighters with the hopeless calm of someone for whom the worst has already happened. She stood beside him and waited until he noticed her.

'Inspector Graham?'

'Yes, sir.' Probably he didn't warrant that any more, but it cost her nothing to say it.

He smiled. He looked terribly weary. Liz didn't know if he'd been told what she'd heard but she thought he knew he was waiting for a body to be recovered. His face and the slump of his erect figure held no hope for Robin's survival. He had already embarked on his grieving; and if there was bound up in it a kind of peace Liz could understand that too. He'd done all in his power for the unquiet spirit that was his son, and it was no wonder if regret at what had happened was tempered by relief at a lifting of the burden. He still had his own problems to work through, and penalties to pay, but there must be some comfort in knowing that nothing like this would happen again.

'I owe so many apologies,' he said softly.

Liz spread a helpless hand. It was dirty and smeared with David Shapiro's blood: she put it quickly behind her back. 'Don't we all?'

He caught her eye. 'Liz, no. You have nothing to regret.'

She hoped he meant that. 'I want to tell you why I acted as I did. Made the decisions I did. I don't want you thinking . . .'

She was finding it harder than she'd expected. She heard herself rambling, took a deep breath and started again, saying what she wanted to in the plainest words she could frame. 'I didn't stop David from attempting a rescue because he was Mr Shapiro's son and Robin was yours. I didn't do it because Robin started the fire. I did it because I believed one dead boy was better than two.'

James Taylor nodded slowly. 'I've done terrible things in the course of this. I've betrayed the trust vested in me. I've betrayed my colleagues. I've permitted an injustice I could have put a stop to. I've lied, cheated and abused my position, and I'm ashamed of it all. I can't honestly say I regret it, because in the same circumstances I don't know that I'd do any different, but I wouldn't like you to think I found it easy.

'With all that,' he went on, watching her expression, 'I only did one stupid thing. I thought that if I got Frank Shapiro out of the way I could cover up Robin's activities. Inspector Graham, you're entitled to feel deeply offended that I put you in charge of an investigation specifically because I believed you'd fail. If it's any comfort to you, if I had this to do again I wouldn't waste my time getting Frank out of my way if it meant dealing with you instead.'

She managed a sad smile. 'I'm sorry things didn't work out better.'

'Yes. Thanks.' He looked away to the flames still visible inside the Mall and sighed. 'I suppose all I can hope for now is that this can be tidied up without anyone else getting hurt.' His eyes came back to her. 'Donovan was injured, wasn't he?'

'Not badly,' said Liz. She was about to mention the woman who'd shielded him but stopped in time. Taylor would hear about that soon enough, there was nothing to gain by adding to his grief now. 'He was already getting stroppy before they took him away in the ambulance.'

For a moment she said nothing more. She was wondering how much authority she had and who she'd have to answer to for exceeding it. She decided there probably wasn't a rule to cover the situation.

She said, 'I don't know if there's any point you staying here. There's Mrs Taylor and your daughter to consider: I imagine it'd be easier for them to hear about Robin from you than from me or anyone else. Why don't you go home? When people need to talk to you I'll know where to send them.'

Taylor looked at the burning building again. She was right: there was nothing to wait for. 'Yes, thank you, I'll do that.' He looked round vaguely, like a man lost. 'My car—?'

'I'll have someone take you,' Liz said quickly. Any time now he'd have to face a new reality with none of the privileges of the old, but she wouldn't let even a disgraced superintendent wander round looking for a way to get home.

'You're very kind,' he said. He smiled. 'I won't be the only one who noticed your effectiveness in these last few days. I hope it'll be recognized officially. I hope your entire department will get some acknowledgement for the job it did. God knows I made it hard enough for you. I wish I'd outwitted you, but I'm proud of the fact that I couldn't.'

He nodded towards the building. 'The people who were in there owe their lives to you. It's going to be a financial disaster, but it would've been a major human tragedy as well except for your insistence that this was the next target. If you hadn't begun the evacuation when you did, Lord knows how many would have died. When the mud starts flying, if any of it comes your way remember that. Your good judgement saved countless lives.'

Liz appreciated that profoundly. For almost the first time in their acquaintance she glimpsed what it was about

248

James Taylor that had made people think he was superintendent material. She regretted not seeing it sooner, or in happier circumstances. But perhaps it was the nature of the man, to shine in defeat. Nothing in his professional life, she thought wryly, became him like the leaving of it.

When there was nothing more she could do at the Mall she returned to Queen's Street. There was already a list on Shapiro's desk of calls to be returned. After she'd rung Brian she made a start on them, beginning with the Assistant Chief Constable.

Halfway down the list she took a breather, leaving the phone off the hook for a minute while she leaned back in Shapiro's chair and closed her eyes. When she opened them again Shapiro was standing in the doorway, silently watching her.

Liz started and went to vacate his desk, but he waved her back. 'Stay there, it suits you.'

She couldn't discern his meaning from his tone. He had no quarrel with her, but perhaps he was too punch-drunk to know that. 'How's David?'

'He'll be all right. He woke up, then he went back to sleep. They're keeping him in tonight but the doctor said he can come home tomorrow.'

'And Donovan?'

'Much the same.'

She waited for him to say something else but he didn't. She set her jaw. She'd rather have left this until tomorrow when they were both a bit less shell-shocked, but if he was nursing a grudge it would be better to get it out in the open. 'Frank, I hope you understand—'

He didn't let her finish. He came forward quickly, took the chair across the desk from hers, leaned forward over his elbows on the scuffed surface. 'Liz, I'm sorry, I'm still firing on three cylinders. Understand? I understand that I owe you more than I can ever repay.

'I'll never forget that you believed in me enough to ignore a direct order from a superior officer. By the book

249

you were wrong: it didn't matter how well you knew me, you should have obeyed orders even if you disagreed with them. But I can't tell you how it feels to know your colleagues have that kind of faith in you. You gave me back my self-respect.

'And tonight you gave me back my son, and I've no words to say what that means to me except that it's more than the other.' For a moment he said nothing more. It was only when she looked up tentatively that she saw he was struggling with tears in his throat. She smiled and reached out for his hand.

'I didn't even know he was missing until the paramedics called me over,' he said. 'When I saw him lying there with the blood pouring out of his head, and you said you'd done that—! Liz, I don't know what I thought but for a moment I wanted to kill you. Afterwards, I was so ashamed. You'd put your whole future on the line because you believed in me, and I couldn't take it on trust that you wouldn't have done that without good reason.'

'There wasn't any other way,' she said softly, still holding his hand. 'I couldn't think of any other way. He'd have gone inside, even knowing what was waiting for him. If we'd struggled he'd have got away from me and gone in anyway. I had to stop him, and the brick was all I had.'

'He owes you his life,' said Shapiro. '*I* owe you his life. Do you want to know something really funny?' She nodded. 'Taylor's terrible crime, which was putting his love for his son ahead of his duty: I'd have done it too. I never knew that till today. But I would. If David had been sick and desperate, I'd have done whatever I had to do to help him. If it'd come to a straight choice between David and Trevor Foot, the poor sod would *still* be in prison.'

Liz shook her head. 'Thank God we'll never know, but I think you'd have found a way out. There aren't too many either/or situations and that wasn't one of them. Taylor didn't leave Foot in gaol to save Robin, he did it to have a hold over you. When he hid that photograph Robin was safe in his clinic in Switzerland. We're entitled to wonder how long he'd have held on to it, or what else he'd have used it for, if the boy had stayed there.'

Shapiro blinked. 'So it wasn't Robin's condition that was responsible for this nightmare, it was my relationship with Taylor? I felt badly enough about putting Foot in jail for somebody else's crime. I don't feel much better to think he'd have been out twelve months ago except that my superintendent considered me too clever by half.'

'He knew he couldn't bully you or bribe you,' Liz said. 'He knew if he ever needed you off his back he'd have to frame you. On mature reflection, I could consider that a compliment.'

Shapiro thought about it. Slowly the creased face relaxed into a grin. He looked about the office, vaguely, as if it looked different from this side of the desk. When his eye found the filing cabinet he got up and came back with a bottle and two glasses. 'Strong liquor is the bane of the detecting classes,' he pronounced solemnly. 'In order to appreciate what a bane it is, you have to be thoroughly conversant with it.'

'I trust I know my duty,' she replied stiffly.

'*L'chaim*,' said Shapiro.

Liz knew another toast. She lifted her glass, made a game stab at a kind of border raider's accent that her Cotswold vocal cords were never designed for. Fortunately, Shapiro's Jewish ears couldn't tell the difference.

'Here's tae us, wha's like us?' she enquired. 'Gey few, and they're a' deid.'

'Perhaps that's just as well,' murmured Shapiro.

ALLISON & BUSBY CRIME

Jo Bannister
A Bleeding of Innocents
Sins of the Heart

Simon Beckett
Fine Lines

Denise Danks
Frame Grabber
Wink a Hopeful Eye
The Pizza House Crash

John Dunning
Booked to Die

Bob George
Main Bitch

Russell James
Slaughter Music

H. R. F. Keating
A Remarkable Case of Burglary

Ted Lewis
Get Carter
GBH
Jack Carter's Law
Jack Carter and the Mafia Pigeon

Ross Macdonald
The Barbarous Coast
The Blue Hammer
The Far Side of the Dollar
Find a Victim
The Galton Case
The Goodbye Look
The Lew Archer Omnibus Vol 1
The Lew Archer Omnibus Vol 2
Meet Me at the Morgue
The Ivory Grin

The Moving Target
Sleeping Beauty
The Underground Man
The Way Some People Die
The Wycherly Woman
The Zebra-Striped Hearse

Margaret Millar
Ask for Me Tomorrow
Mermaid
Rose's Last Summer
Banshee
The Murder of Miranda
A Stranger in My Grave

Sax Rohmer
The Fu-Manchu Omnibus Vol I

Richard Stark
Deadly Edge
The Green Eagle Score
The Handle
Point Blank
The Rare Coin Score
Slayground
The Sour Lemon Score

Donald Thomas
Dancing in the Dark

Marilyn Wallace (ed.)
Sisters in Crime

I. K. Watson
Manor
Wolves Aren't White

Donald Westlake
Sacred Monsters
The Mercenaries
The Donald Westlake Omnibus